Practical Contract Management

Ray Carter
Steve Kirby
Alan Oxenbury

Cambridge Academic

Printed and bound in the United Kingdom by
4edge Ltd, 7a Eldon Way Industrial Estate, Hockley, Essex, SS5 4AD.

Contents

Foreword

Contract management has steadily become recognized as a critical business discipline. The volatility of today's business conditions and the increasing complexity of trading relationships have combined to raise the importance of both risk and relationship management. Contracts – and the contracting process – are fundamental to these capabilities.

But as various bodies (ranging from The Economist, to the UK's National Audit Office, to President Obama) have observed, most organizations today are not very good at contract management. And that is why this book is an important addition to the development of skills and knowledge in the field.

Today, Contracting faces demands to be a source of innovation and to ensure flexibility in supply relationships, while also guarding against reputation risks. Good contracts provide a mutually accepted base for the supply relationship. But more importantly, they offer a tool for governance of the post-award delivery and relationship.

Today's markets are increasingly characterized by frequent change. This may be due to economic volatility, to regulatory change, to natural disasters or to the pace of technical innovation – but in combination, these influences mean that our trading relationships are subject to unprecedented levels of unpredictability. This demands that the next phase of Contracting maturity – and organizational value – will come from mastery of contracting and relationship management.

This book is not about the strategic aspects of contracting. Instead, it offers the practitioner a practical guide and insights to the basics of contract management. and is therefore an invaluable primer for the individual professional who wishes to build their personal skills and capabilities.

Tim Cummins is CEO of The International Association for Contract & Commercial Management (IACCM) which is a global non-profit organization that unites both buy-side and sell-side contracting and commercial professionals in a mission to improve the success and value of trading relationships.

Tim Cummins, CEO of The International Association for Contract & Commercial Management (IACCM)

Preface

This book is about Contract Management. As a subject, this has tended to be viewed as being very much the junior partner in the procurement cycle or the part of the process that is somebody else's problem. There are many first class texts on how to manage the procurement cycle right up to the award of contract and this textbook in no way attempts to compete with them. We are attempting to fill a perceived gap in the general literature by giving some practical advice to those who are responsible for managing contracts, but struggle to find a single textbook covering the subject.

All too often, once the contract has been placed, there has been an expectation that somehow the contract will manage itself. Supposedly all the hard work in issuing invitations to tender and evaluating bids and carrying out negotiations has been completed and the most economically advantageous or best value for money bid has been selected. This is entirely right and proper, but fails to recognise that professional contract management can also bring about significant cost savings, quality, delivery improvements and innovations to products, services or business processes.

This book covers both the hard and soft issues regarding contract management. As well as looking at for example how to hold an inaugural meeting or deal with a contractual claim, we also discuss the nature of the relationship with the contractor, looking at both adversarial and collaborative models as well as measures you might take to motivate the contractor.

The book is written from the standpoint of getting it right first time; we view good contract management as a positive adding value process. Nevertheless the book does not shy away from the fact that things do and will go wrong and therefore there are also chapters on dispute resolution and legal issues that might affect the individual managing the contract.

It is clear from reports from government bodies and private sector research, that there is scope for substantial savings through good contract management. It is a professional discipline that should be carried out by professionals, which should lead to better contractor performance.

Ray Carter, Steve Kirby, Alan Oxenbury

Introduction to Contract Management & Administration

Definitions

What is Contract Management?

Contract management is the process that ensures both parties to a contract fully understand their respective obligations and that these are fulfilled as efficiently and effectively as possible to provide the best value for money.

This gives the impression of a "adversial" approach to contract management, The role of the contract manager is almost supervisory in nature, ensuring the contractors meet their "obligations".

A good example of the issue of obligations is the recent Atkins case. The organisation denied the claim that contracts represent poor value for money. The company provides a 24-hour accommodation helpdesk and IT platform for the UK Probation Service estate. "This involves the handling of calls, the provision of an asset management system and a works approval and instruction process to the service's contractors," a spokesman for the supplier said. "We are meeting our obligations under this contract."

A Contrasting Definition

We would subscribe to the more modern, enlightened and progressive interpretation of contract management.

Contract management is a process by which a contractor is motivated, enabled and empowered to achieve extra value added, over and above that which has been specified originally and assessable against criteria in the original contract. This extra added value can include process innovation, cost reduction and service improvement. The emphasis is this definition is on the contractor as an asset rather than a liability. Another key issue is that the process should be to the benefit of both parties.

For example this approach adopted by BAE Systems and its contractors helped the defence giant unveil the UK's first unmanned military combat aircraft recently. The £142.5 million programme to build the Taranis vehicle has included supplier investment of around £30 million and was delivered through a partnership deal between BAE Systems, Rolls-Royce, QinetiQ, GE Aviation and the UK's Ministry of Defence. Another definition of Contract management is the active management of the relationship between the client and the contractor over the term of the contract for the provision of goods and services to the agreed standards. This again relates to the relationship aspect.

The Office of Government Commerce (OGC) defines Contract management as:

"The phase of the procurement cycle in which a supplier delivers the required goods or services in accordance with a procuring authority's specification".

The OGC also makes the point that contract management should be proportionate to the value, risk and complexity of the contract and goes on to highlight some of the benefits of effective contract management include:

- More favourable contract outcomes.

- Improved quality of service and customer focus.

- Achieving value for money and financial control.

- Decrease in the level of risk.

- Clarification of roles and responsibilities of the contract manager, contractors, end users.

- Early identification and resolution of poor performance, other problems or disputes.

- Evaluation of the specification against contract performance and identification of contract changes or variations.

Issues of complexity and risk, along with nature of the contract and their effect upon the contract management process are covered later in the book.

The Chartered Institute of Purchasing and Supply (CIPS) Definition

Contract life cycle management "is the process of systematically and efficiently managing contract creation, execution and analysis for maximising operational and financial performance and minimising risk."

The Foundations of Effective Contract Management

The good practice contract management framework developed by the UK government referrers to the four blocks of good contract management. These are:

Structure and resources, delivery, development, and strategy – and these comprise of 11 areas organisations should consider when planning and delivering contract management, together with the key activities that fall under each of the 11 areas (see figure 1 overleaf):

> **Figure 1: Key Areas**
>
> - Planning and governance
> - Market management
> - People
> - Supplier relationship management
> - Administration
> - Supplier development
> - Good practice framework
> - Relationships
> - Contract development
> - Performance
> - Risk
> - Payment

Contract Management in Context

The guidance goes on to say state that some of the key issues that can influence contract management include the following:

- Whether contract management staff have been involved in the earlier tendering/contract award phase.

- The style of the tendering process. An adversarial tendering process may lead to a more adversarial or confrontational relationship during the contract management phase, although good working relationships between the staff on both sides who will manage the contract can be developed at the same time that separate, sometimes tough, negotiations are taking place to finalise the contract.

- The 'cultural fit' between customer and supplier. For example, if one party feels comfortable working in a very process-driven, detailed manner, while the other prefers a more open, high-level relationship, then developing successful contract management will be more challenging.

- A contract where one party feels they are disadvantaged by the terms and conditions, or the commercial terms, of the contract may lead to more adversarial contract management.

- Key hard outputs that have a major impact on the design and effectiveness of contract management – such as key performance indicators and service level agreements – are often determined during the tendering/contract award phase.

Role of the Contracts Manager

Tim Cummings, CEO of IACCM, has identified the role and responsibilities of modern contract managers and administrators. His list combines both the administrative, for example including maintaining records and the more strategic and managerial activities. The list includes:

- Contract Drafting.

- Evaluation, Negotiation and Execution.

- Serve as the point of contact for customers on contractual matters. Act as contractual "middleman" between company employees and customers, ensuring timely review and approval/reconciliation of variations.

- On all standard and non standard contracts, provide redlined recommendations and often negotiate directly with our customer's attorneys or purchasing staff until consensus has been reached.

- Maintain contractual records and documentation such as receipt and control of all contract correspondence, customer contact information sheets, contractual changes, status reports and other documents for all projects.

- Provide guidance on contract matters to project managers, including training to new project managers and other employees in contracting procedures.

- Develop and implement procedures for contract management and administration in compliance with company policy. As appropriate, contribute to or influence company policies.

- Monitor compliance by company employees with established procedures.

- Work with Risk Management Department to coordinate contractual insurance requirements.

- Work with Finance to ensure adherence to broader finance and risk requirements such as revenue recognition, pricing and discounting policies, export controls etc. This may include 'financial engineering' and understanding/evaluating economic impact of terms and term options.

- Support Product Management/Marketing to ensure company products and services are offered with appropriate, competitive terms and conditions.

- Monitor competitive terms. Monitor customer satisfaction with our terms and conditions and contracting practices and recommend changes.

- Ensure that signed contracts are communicated to all relevant parties to provide contract visibility and awareness, interpretation to support implementation.

- Handle on-going issue and change management.

- Monitor transaction compliance (milestones, deliverables, invoicing etc.).

- Oversee Service Level Agreement Compliance.

- Ensure contract close-out, extension or renewal.

He goes on to state that the emphasis within this list will vary. For example, some groups have little or no responsibility up to the point of contract signature; and others little or no role after signature (though there is a marked trend towards consolidation of pre- and post-responsibilities within the same group).

Reporting line also makes a difference, with groups reporting to legal tending to have a narrower set of tasks (potentially little responsibility for non-legal aspects of the contract or related policies and procedures, especially in terms of any financial accountability). Geography has certainly been a major factor in the past, with few Contract Managers visible in non-Common Law countries. However, this is also changing as business globalizes and contract forms and procedures grow more consistent.

Contract management can therefore be said to consist of a combination of roles and responsibilities. However, the main task areas are consistently service delivery management, relationship management and contract administration. Who carries out these functions depends on the nature and scale of the contract. However, it is likely that there will be, as a minimum, a nominated individual responsible for managing the contract on the customer side and one on the provider side.

Contract Administration

The effective and efficient administration of contracts is critical to the overall success of any contract. The process can include a number of the activities for example maintaining signed copies of contracts and is an important part of the process. We need to have a process to ensure that key trigger points are recorded and action taken, for example contract termination dates.

We also have to have a process whereby regular reports and (indeed ad hoc reports) of transactions, issues, events etc. are produced as management information and distributed to appropriate stakeholders in the process of contract management.

Contract administration is key to a successful contract close out, whereby the lessons learned from contract execution can be disseminated throughout the organisation.

The Contract

Contracts, as a key document in the process, are a means to build better business partnerships and to ensure successful business outcomes. Contract Management Systems enforce well-defined contract procedures, assure clear allocation of roles and responsibilities and establish a proactive execution environment. IT contract management system will reduce risk of non-performing suppliers and provide efficiency gains by:

- increasing contract visibility across the business.

- eliminating the need for disparate systems and redundant workflows.

- reducing contract cycle times.

- enabling collaboration across the enterprise.

- providing top- and bottom-line results.

Nature of Contract Management and Administration

If we compare the nature of the activities associated with both contract management and contract administration then we can see that the differences are fundamental, yet without efficient contract administration, then effective contract management becomes very difficult, if not impossible.

Contract Management	Contract Administration
Relationship focus	Operational focus
Strategic	Tactical
Process development	Process compliance
Longer term time frame	Short term/transactional
Holistic view	Narrow focus
Driven by added value	Driven by key performance indicators

Symptoms of Poor Contract Management

In many organisations contracts are not well managed or administered and as consultants we often come across examples of poor contract management. In the first instance we look for the symptoms of poor practice, the underlying causes can then be better analysed and remedies applied. The symptoms or the observable outcomes include the following:

- Poor or inappropriate scope of work.

- Cost and time over runs.

- Instructions not in writing.
- Conflicts and disputes with stakeholders and contractors.

- Lack of compliance.

- Critical Success Factors not identified.

- HSE issues.

- Excessive use of variations.

All of these are common expressions of a lack of a robust and fit for purpose process combined with less than competent people. The specific causes of poor performance can include a poor contractor selection process, lack of key stakeholder involvement, poor contract execution and focus on price and not total life cycle costs. These issues will addressed later in the book.

The Organisational Model of Contract Management

A recent study conducted by the IACCM entitled the *Organizational Models and Reporting Study Survey* drew input from 481 participants across a wide range of industries and regions.

The study explored how companies deliver contract and commercial services to the business. The study found that the majority have implemented a centralized model, although there are noticeable variations between industries and geographies.

Centralization is more common for procurement than it is for sales contracting. An overwhelming majority of practitioners perceived centralization to offer benefits – a marked change from the findings of past surveys, which indicated strong resistance to the consolidation of resources, with a belief that it would lead to a loss of flexibility and responsiveness to business/customer needs. The main findings included:

- 48% of businesses have comprehensive cross- business coverage of dedicated contract management resources for both buy-side and sell-side operations.

- 35% of participants on the sell side and 44% on the buy side responded that all contracts personnel have a single central reporting line. The most centralized industry is Technology/Software with 53% on the sell side and 64% on the buy side.

- Reporting lines are varied. 56% on the buy side report within procurement. On the sell side, the highest proportion (34%) report to Legal. A Legal reporting line is most common in Aerospace and Defence, Services and Outsourcing, Technology and Software and Telecommunication.

- 94% of the participants responded that centralization is beneficial.

Survey participants reported that the top three benefits achieved through a centralized contract/commercial management organization are:

- More consistency in handling customers or suppliers.

- Improved contract compliance.

- Improving the management of risk.

- It could be said that this shift is driven by the recession and the need for all types of organisations to control costs and extract extra added value from all of its contracts. These finding also indicate a distinctive shift to a more centralised and perhaps higher profile for the contract management process and professionals.

Summary

In this chapter the following key areas were covered:

- Definitions of what contract management and administration are, as critical business processes.

- How the context of risk, value and complexity can affect the process and profile of contract management.

- The role of the contract managers and their responsibilities.

- The organisational model for managing contracts.

Case Study

Alpha Engineering recently embarked upon a programme of refurbishment of its main office block. This was a major contract with an estimated expenditure of $4m. The Engineering Manager felt that the contract should be managed by his team, given that the work could impact upon his operations. The Head of Facilities Management had other ideas. He was sure that the contract should be under his direct control. The Engineering Manager realises that finance needs to be involved, but perceives this is purely a bookkeeping role and cannot see value in them being closely involved.

A contract team kick-off meeting has been set up and cancelled several times before and the interested parties finally met. At this meeting there is some disagreement about what the term "facilities" actually mean and indeed what is meant by "refurbishment". A long and complex debate ensued. In the meantime the Head of Facilities Management has asked Delta contractors (see figure 2) to have a look at the project and given an indication of time and cost to undertake the work.

Figure 1

Delta Ltd

Company Profile:

Small local maintenance contractor owned by Peter Jones and his son David. The company has a small team of full time employees, plus access to a network of sub-contractors. The company was formed only 2 years ago and has undertaken several small-scale refurbishment contracts.

Current Financial Details:

Debtors	£50,000.00
Creditors	£95,000.00
Stock	£30,000.00
Cash	£2,000.00
Turnover	£300,000.00
Profit /Loss	(£10,000.00)

Outstanding Disputes

Claim against Delta by XXT Ltd for poor quality work and non-performance.

The scope of work given to Delta is very vague. The Engineering Manager believes (even though he has no previous experience of managing contracts) he is able to ensure that the work does not interfere with the next planned office move, due to take place shortly. He believes the work will only last a few weeks and should not therefore cause any problems. Delta has no experience of working in this environment and has based their estimates upon similar contracts they have undertaken at a nearby hospital. To them refurbishment means the 3 "R"s, that is "repair, re-paint and replace". The time and cost estimates produced by Delta are well under the $4 m estimated by the Commercial Contracts Manager. The FM Manager sees an opportunity to cut costs and reduce the time taken to achieve completion.

In the meantime the Head of Staff Welfare is becoming more and more concerned about the poor staff facilities at the Alpha office and the risk of a major drop in staff morale is a risk. He feels obliged to send a memo to the Head of Facilities Management expressing his concerns. In response to this, the FM Manager verbally instructs Delta Contracts to commence work, which do next day.

> **Task**
> What are the potential problems that could arise in the future management of this contract?

- No single point of contractual control within Alpha could lead to miscomm and confusion within the company.
- Lack of experienced contract management could lead to delays and poor value for money
- Poor selection of contractors combined with lack of SLA's and KPI's could lead to poor or unfinished results to the cost of Alpha.

2 An Overview of the Contracting Process

Introduction

One of the most important aspects of effective contract management is to have a thorough knowledge of the basic process of letting and awarding contracting. There are a number of stages through which a contract passes and each one requires attention to ensure that it is successfully completed before the process continues to the next stage. In this chapter we will consider each of these stages. The whole contracting process may be illustrated with a flow diagram, which can be found on page 19.

All contracts will also have stakeholders. These are individuals or groups of individuals who have an interest in a contract, its progression and its successful outcome. They might also have some effect, in some cases not inconsiderable, on the contract's performance and outcome. Because of this, stakeholders need to be kept informed and 'managed' at every stage of the contract's progression.

The following checklist was developed by Ray Carter and was published in *Supply Management* in May 2009. The article identified six key questions that need to be addressed as the start of any contracting process.

It should be noted that the criteria used in this checklist must be considered and established before the process commences because they all involve a degree of pre-analysis of what is required to be achieved by the contract.

- The first question that needs to be addressed is have we fully defined what we mean by **"Success"**? This may include time and cost metrics, but can also include innovative outcomes, customer satisfaction and sustainability to name but a few. The point is that we must have a clear idea of what we value and want to achieve, this provides focus and direction to all concerned. The need for UK Local Government to reduce the time from OJEU notice to contract award by 10% can be regarded as a clear definition of success.

- The second question is do we really have **"Stakeholder engagement?"** For a contract to be efficiently and effectively executed there must be an appropriate degree of consultation with and participation in by the key stakeholders in the process of contract strategy development. Failure to engage will no doubt lead to inappropriate specifications, gaps between needs and outcomes. Often major problems with contract execution occur down stream in the contracting life cycle when issues that were not raised at the outset suddenly become apparent. The need to map stakeholders in terms of project support and understanding of the project and thus identifying the advocates, blockers, followers and opponents is critical to the process. The skills of persuasion and influencing need to be deployed by the team to ensure full engagement.

- The third question asks whether we have created a **"Shared Vision?"** of what is required by all the key stakeholders, developing a common understanding of what is required, the costs and time scales involved and the resources required.

- The development of an appropriate **"Specification"** (or scope of work) comes next and is critical to ensure successful contract execution. The type of specification (performance/functional/technical) needed is of course dependent upon a number of factors, including the nature of the service, its complexity and the maturity of the supply market. The key issue in terms of successful contract execution is that the contractor fully understands what is required by the client and therefore the role of the specification as medium of communication is crucial. In many instances specifications are created to impress peer groups, rather than communicate a clear fit for purpose to those who have to deliver the outcomes.

- The need for a robust and coherent contracting **"Strategy"** could be said to be at the heart of effective execution, DPSS Consultants have developed a simple model of contract strategy development which includes analysis, choices, type of contract, strategy acid test, effective implementation and measurement of value. The key questions we ask here relate to the "acid test". Is the strategy suitable in terms of our needs, structure, core competences and risk appetite? Is it acceptable to our stakeholders, do we have their buy-in? Is it feasible, bearing in mind our resources and required timelines?

- Next is the need to ensure we have a **"Suitable"** type of contract in place, supported by a robust contract management system. Fixed price, time and materials, cost plus reimbursable, day rates and target cost (to name but a few) all have their place, often combined together. The key question is what determines fit for purpose? In some instances the option is determine by the nature of the work, often maintenance contracts are time and materials based. Factors such as risk, contract value, relationship with the contractor, speed of mobilisation and project complexity all need to be taken into account.

Once we have addressed these key questions, then a robust contract management system can takeover to manage the process of execution. Contract management is the critical process by which a contractor is motivated, enabled and empowered to achieve extra value added, over and above that which has been specified originally and is assessable against criteria in the original contract. Successful contract execution is often characterised by the active participation of those who will actually manage and administer the contract, prior to contract award.

The UK Office for National Statistics has suggested an in-house team should be used to carry out procurement and that contract management should be at the heart of the project from the outset, ONS chief procurement officer Scott Howell told *Supply Management* – "Engaging suppliers early on in the process can ensure the requirements are fully understood, as well as having the amount of risk and change reduced," he said.

The Contracting Process

As mentioned above, the actual contracting process is extremely important and understanding it provides the basis for measuring performance in the contract. If the contracts officer measures contractor performance at each stage in the contracting process, if there are any problems identified, they can work with the contractor to take corrective action so that the remainder of the contract should reach a satisfactory conclusion. Equally, if there are no specific problems but performance is 'below par', the contracts officer can use the measurement information to work with the contractor to develop and improve future performance.

A diagrammatic view of the contracting process is shown in figure 2.1 and there follows a brief explanation of each of the stages in the diagram. We should note, however, that some of these stages are explained in more detail in chapters that follow.

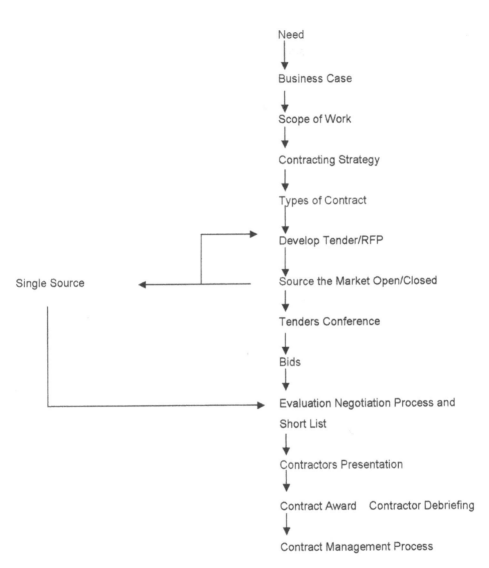

Figure 2.1 Contracting Process

Need

This is the first stage of any contract process: the identification of the basic need for whatever it is that the contract will ultimately provide. At its most basic level this can be simply identifying that something that is usually kept in stock, for example nuts and bolts, is about to run out and therefore requires re-ordering.

Such contracts, however, rarely need 'managing' in the true sense of the word but the same basic principle may be applied to more complex issues. For example, suppose that a departmental manager believed that a new IT system complete with Intranet and Extranet would be beneficial to the organisation as a whole and to their department in particular. This would be identification of a need.

Business Case

When a need has been identified, the next stage is to present a business case for it. This involves the individual(s) that has identified the need putting together a presentation to the organisation's senior management to justify proceeding with the contract. Such a presentation would usually include an explanation of benefits that would accrue from the purchase of the product/equipment/service that is envisaged. Such benefits should be fully justified in terms of value that might be added to the organisation's processes or systems or, if it is likely, that might be added to the organisation's finished product or service that it provides for customers.

As well as forecast benefits, the business case should include a summary of possible drawbacks that might accrue from the contract's implementation or risks that might be attached to its implementation. The identification of risks will be covered later in the chapter but in summary, the purpose of risk identification at the earliest stage should allow the development of strategies designed to remove or reduce the impact of such risks should they occur.

Scope of Work

This refers to the specification of the work (product/equipment/ service) that has been deemed to be required. It should be as technically complex as it needs to be in order to inform potential contractors as to exactly what they need to supply or, at the very least, to help them put a bid together for the contracts officer to analyse and evaluate at the tendering stage. As said, this can be a very complex process and it will be covered in more detail in chapter 3.

Contracting Strategy

When we are considering awarding large contracts that might be long-term, as opposed to minor, low-value, short-term contracts, we need to develop a strategy that will define such aspects as how we intend to find a suitable contractor, how we intend to award the contract and how we intend to manage its performance. Any other important aspects such as performance measurement methods should also be included. Contracting strategy might involve such aspects as examining supply market options to address critical business issues such as growth, innovation, HSE, generation of income and achieving synergies via unblocking or protecting key leverage points along the value chain.

It is recommended that organisations should develop a contracting strategy based on the following.

- Analysis of organisational plans by identifying and measuring in qualitative terms, (e.g. core or non-core), the importance of each activity to the organisation and the key characteristics of the services, works, materials and equipment required for each activity. It is also essential to consider the nature of the supply market from which they are sourced and opportunities for total cost improvement.

- Identification of the activities currently being undertaken in the contracting process and comparison with those required in future to support the organisation's objectives and formulation of a contracting strategy based on this analysis.

- Evaluation of the systems and skills necessary to implement the contracting strategy and development of options to overcome any shortcomings in these important areas.

- Consideration of the extent of contracting out (outsourcing). It is important to ensure that there is a 'business need' for a particular package of work or service to be contracted out. There has to be a real 'dividend' in allowing contractors to tender for works and services which can just as economically be obtained from internal resources. The reliance on contractors can also severely weaken the technical knowledge base of the company.

- Identification of members of staff responsible for carrying out the contracting policies.

- Setting of targets and development of measurements for monitoring the progress of the implementation of the contracting strategy. For example, are the benefits derived from the contracting strategy better or worse than expected?

- In order to ensure the participation of all relevant functions, the contracts team should enlist the explicit support of the senior management team for this process.

Types of Contract

There is a variety of types of contract and we need to consider which one would be best for the type of work that is required. The different types of contract will be covered in more detail in chapter 6 but here is a brief outline of them:

- **Time and Materials Work (Day works):** this is a contract arrangement under which the contractor charges for resources (labour, plant and materials) actually used in carrying out the work at agreed rates for labour/staff and agreed on-costs for plant and materials. It can be used where the requirement cannot be determined or specified in detail as well as where requesting a fixed lump sum price would result in an unacceptable level of risk being borne by the contractor, which would be reflected by a high price because of the necessary contingency.

- **Cost reimbursable contract:** here the contractor is paid on the basis of ascertained and proven costs expended in the performance of the contract. This would include agreed management costs and overheads as well as a predefined rate of profit. This type of contract may be employed in circumstances where there is significant uncertainty in the contract; in particular where:
  - the scope of work is relatively unknown
  - the possibility of significant indefinable emergent work is apparent
  - timescales are difficult or impossible to define.

The aim of the contract should be the alignment of the interests of both client and the contractor to ensure that the work is completed timely and efficiently and that the contractor should earn a reasonable profit.

Contract requirements are often such that the extent of the scope of work is uncertain and this creates the need for varying degrees of flexibility being incorporated into the structure of the contract. This can be achieved in many ways depending on the circumstances although three in particular are most often used by:

- Having some flexibility in the established lump sums;

- Establishing some form of cost reimbursement.

- **'Re-measurement' contracts:** establishing agreed rates which cover the range of possible work scope but are then either called-off as the true work emerges or measured against actual usage during and at the end of the work.

Developing the Invitation to Tender

The invitation to tender (ITT) package must be constructed so as to inform potential contractors of what is required in as much detail as possible so that they may submit a meaningful bid. This will then allow the contracts officer, possibly in conjunction with a team, to analyse the bids and select the 'best' contractor based on the bids.

All required details must be included in the tender document because if this is not done it increases the possibility of contractors submitting bids that are not meaningful. his will include the scope of work, contract terms and conditions and instructions to tenders regarding the form of the tender and the timescales.

Request for Quotation (RFQ) or Request for Proposal (RFP).

The purpose of these is to enable the contracts officer to carry out a process whereby a number of potential contractors may submit bids (quotations) for the contract. Often these are in the form of a performance based outline scope of work. This has the advantage enabling the contracts officer the opportunity to source the supply market for innovation and best practices, without the issue of formal offer and acceptance.

Source the market

As in any contracting process, once the requirement has been ascertained and developed, the market must be sourced in order to identify suitable potential contractors. Some would say that this should be as many suitable contractors as possible. This process involves scouring the supply market using tools such as the Internet to find companies that might be able to supply the requirement. It might also involve a tendering process (sending RFQ/RFPs to potential contractors) such as that referred to in the previous section.

This important element of sourcing/tendering might be carried out as an 'open' process where any company that believes it could fulfil the contract may bid or as a 'closed' process where only chosen companies are permitted to bid. Such companies ('potential contractors') must then be appraised ('pre-qualified') to ascertain that, if the contract were awarded to them, they would be able to perform it to the required level of quality and/or service. This process is covered in more detail in chapters 4 and 5.

Single Source

In some situations, it is seen as an alternative to tendering because it is apparent that there is only one contractor available that could fulfil the contract, in the case or Original Equipment Manufacturer (OEM) This might also be as a result of the sourcing process only revealing one source or arising from prior market knowledge of the individual or team responsible for carrying out the sourcing and contract award process. It could be that there is the need for a very large contractor (leader in the field) to carry out an assignment or an emergency has arisen.

Some experts recommended the issue of formal tender documents in single source contracting situations, and to commence negotiations only after receipt of a formal bid.

Tenders Conference

Before bids are submitted by contractors, best practice contracting organisations hold a tenders conference. This is a meeting to which all potential bidders are invited with a view to being given guidance as to the contract's requirements as well as asking questions relevant to the contract and/or the tendering process. The purpose of this is that all tenderers have a complete picture of the contracting organisation's requirements, which should allow them to present robust and meaningful tenders

Bids

The next stage is for potential contractors that are interested in being awarded the contract will submit a detailed bid for evaluation by the contracts officer.

Evaluation, Negotiation Process and Short List

After all of the bids have been received (usually by no later than a specified date and time) they must be evaluated by the contracts officer, possibly together with other important decision makers in the contracting organisation, to ascertain which potential contractor is providing the best bid and is therefore, the one most likely to be awarded the contract. Alternatively, the intention might only be to create a short list, with final contractor selection taking place at a later stage. Such bid evaluation is often carried out by a small committee so that a number of relevant points of view may be used as part of the evaluation process.

Many contracts officers then find it useful to carry out post tender negotiation with, usually, the 'best' 2 or 3 bidders or whatever number of bidders has been placed on a short list. The purpose of this is to clarify any queries that might arise from the bids and/or to try to persuade the bidder to improve certain aspects of the bid. In this latter respect, there have certainly been situations over time where (say) the 2nd best bidder has become the 'best' bidder after post tender negotiation.

Clearly, in single source situations, there would be no post tender negotiation but it would be usual to negotiate an agreement with the single source prior to contract award. Equally, for major contracts, even if post tender negotiation does not take place as such, it would be usual to negotiate with the contractor chosen through the tendering process in order to agree a legally-binding agreement that both parties are comfortable with. This process will be covered in more depth in chapter 5.

Tenderers' presentation

If the contract has not been awarded as the immediate result of the tendering process or post tender negotiation and/or the contract is extremely important (as well as likely to be expensive), it can be useful to ask the potential contractors on the short list to make a presentation to a management team comprising key decision makers in the contracting organisation. The purpose of this is so that the potential contractors may be questioned about (e.g.) technical aspects of how they intend to perform the contract and may explain details of how they intend to perform it. It can be particularly useful, at this stage, to encourage the potential contractors to be proactive in terms of their approach to the performance of aspects of the contract.

When these presentations have been made, a decision may be made by the contracting organisation as to which potential contractor will be awarded the contract.

Contract Award and Contractor Debriefing

Final contract award will be made to the potential contractor that has indicated by means of the tender process, post tender negotiation and possibly, presentation as mentioned above. It is usual to negotiate contract details and (e.g.) terms and conditions so that an agreement, once reached, will be legally binding. Any such agreement should leave both sides in no doubt as to what is required of them in terms of contract performance and how the contract will be managed.

At this stage, it is also useful to debrief unsuccessful tenderers to provide some idea of why they were unsuccessful. This action should mean that such tenderers may gain insight into how they could improve their bids/tenders in future, which would be useful for them but might also mean that they might become more competent bidders if we use a similar tendering process again in the future for similar contracts. This topic will be covered in more depth in chapter 5.

Contracting Process

Once the contract has been awarded, the contractor will start to perform.

The contractor's performance should always be measured to ascertain that they are giving we what we require and/or to identify aspects of the performance that could be improved. If the contractor is not providing what is required, we would need to take steps to ensure that their performance is brought into line with our requirements. Specific problem resolution could also form part of the contracting process. This process will be covered in much greater depth in chapter 7.

Stakeholder Management

It is important to recognise that there are a number of individuals or groups of individuals that will have an interest in the contract being awarded. These people might also have some influence over the way in which the contractor is chosen, the contract awarded and performed including its progress and completion. They are known collectively as 'stakeholders'.

Because of the influence that stakeholders could have on all aspects of a contract from the initial stages of identifying the need, developing a business case, etc. through to actual management of the contract, they must be communicated with and involved in the progress of the contract to a greater or lesser extent. We should note, however, that the amount of interest in and influence over, a contract that stakeholders have will depend entirely on their position in, or relationship to, the contracting organisation.

Who is a stakeholder?

There is a natural inclination to minimise the numbers included in the category of 'stakeholder'. The more stakeholders there are, the greater is the task of communication, engagement, consideration and management. Nevertheless, it is a risk-laden approach to wilfully overlook any organisation or individual having the position or desire to pose a problem at a later stage of the process.

The contracting organisation needs to ask itself the following questions in order to identify the stakeholders in a contract and begin the process of management by plotting the ways in which they may engage with the planned project:

- Who are our stakeholders?
- What are their stakes (interest in the contract; influence over it)?
- What opportunities and challenges are presented to us?
- What responsibilities (economic, legal, or from the

perspective of corporate social responsibility (CSR)) do we have to all these stakeholders?

- What strategies or actions should we take to best deal with stakeholder challenges and opportunities?

There is bound to be a large list of stakeholders. It will usually be appropriate to identify them in two main divisions – those internal to the organisation, (e.g.) shareholders and those from the broader environment, (e.g.) government. In each case they can be further categorised in terms of their level of interest and their power to disrupt or promote the future venture. Mendelow (1991) described a matrix for handling this information:

	Level of Interest	
	Low	High
Low	**Category A** Minimal effort	**Category B** Keep informed
High	**Category C** Keep satisfied	**Category D** Key player

(Power is the vertical axis: Low / High)

The extent to which stakeholders affect the activities of an organisation such as contract award and management depends on the relationship between the stakeholder and the organisation. Mendelow's matrix provides a way of mapping stakeholders based on the power to affect the organisation and their interest in doing so. It identifies the responses which management needs to make to the stakeholders in the different quadrants. The nature of the stakeholders that fit into each box of the matrix will depend entirely on the nature of the contract but examples might be as follows:

Those with high interest and high power ('key players'): typically, these would be senior managers and internal customers (or external customers if the contract is one that would affect them directly such as a contract for the provision of transport of goods). Any stakeholder in this group needs to be involved and informed as to progress, of problems, etc. on a constant basis by means of regular meetings and communication. This would be the case especially if an unforeseen problem occurred.

Those with high interest and low power: such stakeholders might be the organisation's employees (although their power would depend on such matters as the strength of any trade union active in the organisation) and the local community in the organisation's location. The latter group's interest would depend on such matters as whether the contract would have any direct effect on them: a contract relating to transport that might increase the number of heavy lorries in the area of the organisation's premises would create high interest, for example. Such stakeholders need to be kept informed of progress and of any benefits/problems that might arise from the contract. This could be achieved by holding meetings regularly but not necessarily frequently – every three months, for example – or by means of regular newsletters.

Those with low interest and high power: these might include shareholders and central government. It might seem strange to say that shareholders have low interest but if the contract is fairly 'run-of-the-mill' or is merely part of the normal running of the organisation, it is unlikely that they would have any special interest in it. Similarly, central government would only have any real interest if the organisation were a major public body and the contract in question were capable of affecting the lives of a large number of people. Such stakeholders should be kept satisfied.

This might include holding occasional meetings such as annually – in the case of shareholders this would happen anyway – where any concerns can be addressed and progress reports made. This assumes that the contract is fairly long term. Another possibility for management of this group would be to ensure that any queries made by stakeholders perceived to be in this category were answered swiftly and in a meaningful way.

Those with low interest and low power: the general public would be the group that stands out here. Minimal effort is required with this group and the standard way of dealing with them is to have a website that can be accessed easily. This could contain information as to the progress of the contract.

One thing not to be overlooked in the determining of stakeholder management strategies is that over the life of a project, stakeholders will tend to move in terms of their relative interest and at different stages may acquire or shed power. For example, community engagement may be highly vociferous prior to a Public Inquiry but diminish once planning decisions have been publicly examined and confirmed. We should also be aware that the box of the matrix into which we place a stakeholder is very much a matter of perception: the amount of power and interest we perceive them to have.

Chapter Summary

In this chapter we have considered an overview of the contracting process and the management of stakeholders:

- Contracting is a lengthy process that originates with the perceived need for the contract and ends with the award of a contract to the 'best' contractor. It is after this stage that contracting, the ongoing process of ensuring that the contract progresses smoothly and in accordance with requirements, begins.

- There is usually a potentially large group of stakeholders who will have an interest in the satisfactory conclusion of a contract. We need to be aware, at all times, of what each stakeholder's specific interest will be, how it can be satisfied and how to correct any problems that might occur in this process.

Case Study

Delta is a large international engineering company, based in the UK, The company has a well-developed procurement and contracting process. Alex , who is the head of maintenance needs to commission a series of works to refurbish several of the organisations older warehouses, located in the UK and across Europe.

He expects the value of the contract to be over $2m, this means it should go to the major tender board for approval. Under Delta contracting procedures, he should now develop a full scope of work and a full contract plan for submission to the tender board for their review and recommendation to the CEO. The submission needs to cover issues such as risk, HSE, type of contract and contract duration and terms and a contract award strategy. However, Alex wants to get this work started as soon as possible and has already advised EAU Construction ltd "unofficially" that it will most likely get the contract.

Alex feels that the decision to include EAU Construction ltd is an obvious one and that the whole contracting process is rather a waste of time and money.

He states many people seem to be involved, yet few of which add any real value. He feels that the tender board members are not competent to pass judgement on his technical or commercial proposal.

Alex has approached 5 local companies to participate in the tender process, of which only 3 expressed any interest. Later in the process one of these withdraws and so Alex is left with EAU Construction and ASU Builders Ltd.

His submission to the minor tender board includes:

Scope of Work
Delta has a requirement to refurbish a series of warehouses; this will include some brick work, electrical and other works to be decided on site.

Contract Duration
The contract works could last for many months and the contractor should plan to have resources available for several years, across many sites in the UK and Europe.

Selection Criteria
Both potential contractors are well known to me, both have occasionally undertaken work of a similar nature. I worked for EAU Construction when I was a young graduate manager. ASU Builders is also a sound company and they have had only a few minor HSE incidents in recent years.

Technical Evaluation
The technical evaluation team have reported that both contractors are technically acceptable, EAU scoring 101 and ASU 103, the minimum being 100.

Award Strategy
We have decided to split the contract 10% - 90% and will offer 90% to EAU who have submitted a price of £2.5m and 10% to ASU who have offered £2.3m.

Task
Evaluate the approach adopted by Alex.

Risks, Rewards and Contract Targeting

Introduction

All contracts are awarded with a view to gaining some 'reward' (advantage to the contracting organisation). Such rewards should be well-known at the outset because they will represent the basic objective (s) of the contract. However, contract award often brings risks with it and in this chapter we will consider typical risks that might arise from the development and award of a contract. 'Management' of risks – being aware of them, their potential and developing strategies to reduce their impact – is also very important.

Additionally, we will consider the concept of 'targeting' contracts. This involves being aware of the recipients or beneficiaries of what the contract has to offer. If contracts are 'targeted' appropriately, they are much more likely to have fewer, less serious risks and stand a much better chance of succeeding than might otherwise be the case.

Risk and Reward

When considering contracts and the process of contractor selection, appraisal, negotiation and final contract agreement, we need to be aware that all contracts have risk associated with them but at the same time, have potential reward associated with them. Risk, generally speaking, refers to anything that could go wrong during the contract's lifetime and reward, whilst not necessarily financial, refers to any benefit that the contracting organisation might accrue from entering the contract.

Before setting up and entering any contract, we should be aware of potential risks and rewards that might stem from it. We should also be aware of the extent of risk and reward.

What is risk?

As we stated above, 'risk' refers to anything that might go wrong with the contract process, which we need to try to assess before entering into a contract. Therefore the risk criteria are directly related to wer business drivers, customer markets, technology, government legislation, and a host of other factors affecting the products and services we purchase. Risks can be classified under the following general headings:

- **Commercial Impact:** the fact that, if the risk materialises, the company might lose money and/or reputation, the latter leading, in turn, to reduced sales.

- **Health & Safety & Environment (HSE) issues:** again, these can seriously affect a company's reputation if problems arise during the performance of a contract.

- **Technology:** modern technology can bring many advantages but if it is not thoroughly developed and tested, it can cause many problems and create stoppages in operations while the problem is fixed.

- **Programme:** some contract programmes do not run smoothly with stoppages, quality problems, lack of suitable equipment and many other sources of problems that might halt or slow down a programme. These should be assessed and contingency plans put in place as much as possible before the programme (contract) commences.

- **Supply Market:** the activities and condition of the supply market can cause risks. These might be the risk of contractors going into liquidation or the need of contractors to increase or fix prices to maintain profitability.

A good example of this risk is Unilever and Procter & Gamble (P&G) who have recently been fined 315.2-million Euros (£278-million) by the European Commission for fixing the price of washing powder.

- **Quality:** this has always presented a risk, that of the quality of work not being up to the required standard. If work carried out by a contractor is not up to standard, this can reflect on the contracting organisation with a resultant reduction in sales or reputation.

Specific examples of risk could be:

- **The number of contractors who can supply the product/ service:** if there are few of these, the risk associated with their going into liquidation becomes greater than it otherwise might be. This is not to say that they might be more likely to go into liquidation but that the risk of problems, e.g. of re-sourcing, would be greater if they were to go into liquidation. Also, there is the potential problem that, if the contractor knows that the contracts officer has not much choice of alternative contractors.

- **The criticality of the product/service to our organisation:** what happens if it does not arrive on time?

- **Lead time:** this is particularly risky if it is uncertain or unpredictable. These situations in supplied goods and services can lead to the contracting organisation's lead time being unreliable.

- **Imported goods:** additional elements to consider when importing/using overseas contractors to perform a service:
  - delivery time and delivery methods (see 'late delivery' below)

- **Exchange rates:** change constantly and a trend of falling value of the contracting organisation's currency can mean that the 'real' cost of imported goods increases. An example here would be during the autumn, the value of a Euro compared to the £Sterling increased from around 75p to around £1. This would have meant that a contract worth 1 million Euros at, say, the end of August would have cost £750,000 but would have cost £1,000,000 by the end of the same year. Also taxation issues: overseas governments might increase export taxes or duties without any warning, the effect of which would be to increase the price of the goods being imported suddenly.

- **Political instability:** the possibility of governments being suddenly replaced by a government that does not approve of exports to the West or to the specific contracting organisation. This can apply to countries through which goods are transported as well as to the country of origin of the goods. It should be remembered that civil wars/strife takes place in some parts of the world and that these occurrences can seriously affect the process of importing goods from these parts of the world.

- **Late delivery:** this can apply especially to items coming from overseas with long and difficult journeys between contractor and contracting organisation. If supplied goods are late, this can make delivery of the contracting organisation's product or service late. This is different from the 'lead time' issue mentioned above and refers to situations where the forecast lead time is acceptable but for some reason, a problem occurs and the goods arrive late.

- **Contract/contractor collapse:** this is particularly serious in times of recession and refers to situations where the contracting organisation places a contract with the contractor only to find that the contractor has gone into liquidation after the contract's running time has started. This can be a serious problem because, if it happens, the contracts officer must find a replacement contractor, which, in the case of complex or difficult products or services, can be a lengthy process.

- **Product safety hazard:** this is the risk that products purchased for good reasons can be discovered to have safety problems during operation.

- **Lack of traceability:** this refers to products that have long delivery journeys and whose position in the journey cannot be 'traced' (e.g. by GPS). This can lead to risk of non-delivery.

- **Consequential loss:** this is the risk of items either arriving late or arriving on time but not working properly. The risk is that either of these occurrences might stop the contracting organisation's operations to the point where it has to compensate its customers.

- **Key person:** if the contractor has a 'key person' such as an account manager looking after the contracting organisation's supplies, it is likely that this person will have good knowledge of the organisation and its requirements but if that person leaves the contractor or has an accident, supplies might begin to fail. It is a good idea, with important contracts to try to ensure that the 'key person' has an assistant or 'substitute'.

- **Dependency:** being heavily dependent on a contractor can be problematic because, if the contractor goes into liquidation or experiences the kinds of problems alluded to above, the result can be serious problems for the contracting organisation.

- **Yesterday's technology:** if contractors are supplying items using yesterday's technology, there is likely to be a resultant effect on the contracting organisation. This would most likely be the gaining of a reputation for being old-fashioned and supplying old-fashioned products. This could be damaging even if the 'old-fashioned' products were extremely reliable.

- **Defects:** this is the possibility that goods might arrive with defects that have either occurred because of poor inspection/quality control at the contractor's premises or be due to damage occurring during the journey.

We will consider ways of mitigating or removing ('managing') these risks throughout the book.

The Aberdeen Research Group recently surveyed 315 business managers from across the globe, 72% of whom were in sourcing, supply chain or procurement, to find that risk analysis was one of their "weak links".

Potential Rewards

We have said that there are many risks that might apply to contracts but there are also potential rewards. These can depend upon the nature and value of the contract.

For example a routine gardening contract is unlikely to deliver much in the way of innovation. Here are some of the potential rewards that can be leverage from contracts:

- **Cost reduction:** this one should be fairly obvious but well-sourced products or services with contractors who can reduce costs and therefore, prices, without reducing quality can lead to a reduction in costs in the contracting organisation.

  This is an example of the "opportunity" for reward, in the form of cost savings. The UK Ministry of Justice has failed to understand the cost of its services, states the UK Committee of Public Accounts The Parliamentary committee, which heard evidence from the ministry criticised the ministry's poor financial management in a report recently published. Margaret Hodge MP, the PAC chairperson, said: "If the Ministry of Justice is to minimise the impact on its frontline services of its tough spending settlement, it must fully understand the cost and value of those services. But the ministry and its arm's-length bodies currently lack that detailed information."

  Another example is Surrey County Council in the UK expects to save £10 million by agreeing better deals with its main suppliers. The local authority is asking its major suppliers, who collectively receive £250 million of the authority's£680 million annual budget, to "share the pain" of the economic climate and council funding cuts The council expects its talks with suppliers to deliver rewards of £10 million over 18 months.

- **Quality improvements:** contractors who can supply high-quality goods can help improve the contracting organisation's operations and potentially, the quality of its own product. If the contractor is able to work to improve quality continually, this effect will be even greater.

- **Service improvements:** contractors that can provide good service help keep the contracting organisation's operations and (e.g.) product delivery reliable. If the contractor is able to improve service, it could mean that the contracting organisation's service and delivery would be improved.

- **Innovation/New Product Development (NPD):** contractors who have continual programmes of innovation or NPD can bring the results of these activities to the contracting organisation. This would help the contracting organisation to use such innovations to improve its own product.

- **Developing new markets:** contractors who can provide some of the aspects of the supply process mentioned above (innovation, quality improvement, etc.) can assist the contracting organisation in the development of new markets for its own products or service because these 'supply chain improvements' can, in effect, be passed on.

- **HSE:** contractors who can show that their goods and/ or services comply with the latest HSE regulations can help the contracting organisation to keep up with such regulations.

Procurement targeting

This is a good starting point for the process of estimating potential risk and reward for a contract and a well-established method of ascertaining these variables is the Kraljic matrix.

This model, which has been in circulation for at least 25 years shows the product portfolio within the four boxes, according to spend and risk, i.e.

Routine   = low value, low risk items or services
Leverage   = high value, low risk items or services
Bottleneck = low value, high risk items or services
Critical   = high value, high risk items or services

In consideration of this model, we are only considering the intrinsic merits of the products we buy, not the contractors we buy them from. The model acts as a basis for further consideration of the supply base available to we. In terms of risk, it is contracts with high risk potential that require a good deal of attention to identify risks and similarly, it is likely that high value contracts are the ones that are likely to yield the greatest rewards. We should remember, of course, that 'reward' often relates to added value, which can help to increase profitability, rather than to direct profitability increases such as reduced purchase prices although, of course, in some situations, reward can increase profitability directly.

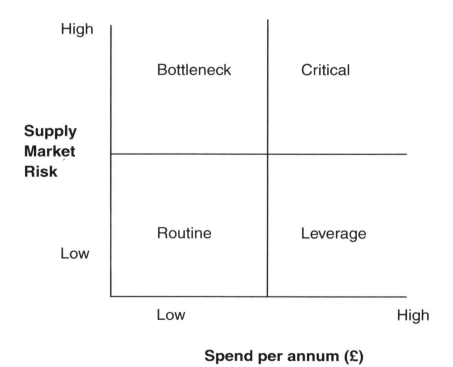

Fig. 2.4: Kraljic matrix

Overview of the Four Procurement Targeting Groups

Routine items

It is unlikely that major contracts or projects will fit into this category although the outsourcing of 'small' services could be included here.

Contracting and supply functions should be administering these items as efficiently as possible. Typical routine items are stationery, fixings and fastenings, and production consumables. Many contracting departments spend large amounts of their time managing these products.

Contracting and supply departments should be concentrating their attention on minimising effort and paperwork and, instead, wherever possible, devolving responsibility to end users. Options may be:

- Set up a call off contract for all the products that will group together then pass back to the budget holder, who will draw product against the contract, at the predetermined prices which contracting has negotiated.

- Arrangements can be made by the contracting function, with contractors, to buy certain items from selected contractors by corporate contracting cards (charge card contracting) thus saving the contracting department time taken placing orders. E-procurement arrangements will, in many organisations, seek to achieve the same end result.

'Routine' solutions

All of these possible solutions are aimed at minimising risk and maximising reward.

- **Long-term relationship (not partnerships, as such):** this should facilitate the development of systems with the contractor that enable the items to be delivered regularly with the minimum of documentation or concern for risk.

- **Cost-of-acquisition focus**, rather than focus on purchase price alone.

- **'Umbrella' contracts (call-off, credit card, e-procurement, direct requisitioning, VMI etc.):** such systems, in effect, 'automate' the contracting process and if they are implemented with contractors with which the purchaser has a good long-term relationship (see above), should mean that the contracting process for such items will operate with the minimum risk. Also, because such systems should mean that contracts officers and other staff need spend little time 'managing' them, there should be reward due to the fact that costs are reduced to a minimum

- **Find a contractor who is small enough to be enthused by our routine business**, or alternatively, a large contractor whose business it is to deliver economies of scale and efficiencies to our routine business. The enthusiastic, small, contractor will work hard to satisfy our requirements meaning that risks should be reduced and rewards maximised. Similarly, the large contractor able to deliver economies of scale will provide a fairly direct reward.

- **Minimal formality**, which can relate to 'umbrella' contracts (see above), could reduce costs and add to rewards by means of (e.g.) the following.
  - no goods-in checking
  - consolidated billing
  - prompt service
  - deliver direct to user/customer

- no stocking
- management reports.

Bottleneck items

Bottleneck items will usually have similarities with 'routine items' the key difference is the greater risk of non-availability and hence the risk, which might be relatively severe, of shortage of supply. The leverage, or negotiating strength, of the purchaser is limited because of the high degree of strength of contractors. The emphasis here is to try and ensure supply. This can be carried out by adopting a long-term relationship incorporating service targets for performance or, alternatively, by adopting a multiple-sourcing strategy, if it is possible to do so, to minimise the risk of over-reliance on any one contractor.

In terms of reward, the likelihood is that this will be low because contractors, typically, will not have a great interest in wer custom when compared with that of other customers and might charge high prices.

Bottleneck solutions

- Try to develop close relationships focusing on how important the contractor/contractor is to the organisation.

- Focus on cost of acquisition, not price.

- Make much effort up-front to ensure that we have the 'best' contractor/contractor possible.

- Long-term contracts, again showing the contractor/ contractor their importance to the organisation.

It is worth commenting that some contracts officers might try to work with internal customers to identify alternative ways of satisfying the need in order to reduce risk and minimise the potential for poor reward. This might involve finding out whether an alternative item, that might be placed in one of the other 'boxes' in the matrix, to that being purchased might perform the function just as well.

Leverage items

Traditionally, the view of leverage items was that the contracting organisation should be exploiting their position, as the contractor market will be competitive and because the purchaser's spend will be one that puts them in a more powerful position with contractors. The leverage box is complex, and the simple exercise of spending power may militate against other objectives, such as rationalising contractors. With these items, the traditional view is that there will usually be many contractors in the supply market meaning that the contracts officer can change contractors easily and quickly if the existing contractor lets them down or is forecast to be about to let them down.

Also, with these items or services, the contracts officer should have much greater negotiation power than with other purchases and should be able to negotiate the lowest prices possible meaning that there would be a direct increase to reward.

Leverage solutions

- Traditional procurement approach; short-term spot buy (although it is worth noting that this is not really relevant to projects, as such).

- Use supply market competition for the initial sourcing exercise and negotiate a sound contractual base. Strict contract terms that, in effect, force the contractor into supplying in ways that suit the contracts officer should have the effect of reducing risk.

It might appear that few, if any, of these solutions would be relevant to projects but, for services/activities falling into this quadrant, there is no reason why we should not adopt some of the above approaches at least at the initial sourcing stage.

Critical items

Critical items will have a high spend on goods/services which have few contractors. A balance can exist between the power of the two parties and the two companies may in fact be dependent on each other. Much will depend on the size of the two organisations.

The choice of contractor strategy can be to pursue a long-term partnership agreement. This can be difficult if the contracting organisation is dealing with a more powerful contractor. Contractors that supply products/services to us in the critical box are the sort of contractors that we wish to invest time and money in, in the form of a contractor development programme, which will include techniques such as:

- Total cost modelling: using (e.g.) open-book costing in order to know the contractor's actual production/provision costs.

- Value analysis and value engineering.

- Continuous improvement, e.g. Kaizen.

Critical solutions

- **Long-term contracting:** this should reduce risk because the contractor is assured of our business and increase reward because we might be able to negotiate good prices based on the contract length and subsequent total quantities purchased.

- **Formal contractual base:** this should be the case in all purchases but is particularly important here. It can reduce risk by ensuring that there are contractual terms that should cover all eventualities.

- Total life costs which might be Life Cycle based and should provide a complete picture of the Total Cost of Operation

(TCO) of the product being purchased. This type of costing usually relates to purchases of major pieces of equipment or of other projects and should help increase reward by enabling the contracts officer to compare the projected TCOs of a number of potential contractors at the tendering/appraisal stages in order to be able to award the contract to the contractor showing the lowest TCO.

- Willingness to share risks and benefits (value engineering, co-make etc.).

It is worth noting that deciding which contractor to purchase from, how to negotiate with them and ultimately cementing the appropriate contractor relationship is not as simple as this segmenting process suggests. Sometimes we are locked into particular relationships; often we are unable to find contractors/contractors who match the ideal. Sometimes, although a contractor is selling something relatively off-the-shelf, their market dominance gives us little power or alternative. Sometimes it is a subjective assessment as to where a particular purchase falls in our market segmentation.

The underlying message of the model is that each product category demands a particular relationship type to be developed if the contracting function is to prosper.

Chapter summary

In this chapter we have considered an overview of risk and reward relating to contracts and ways in which such risks can be assessed and managed.

Contract management is a lengthy process that originates with the perceived need for the contract and ends with the award of a contract to the 'best' contractor. It is after this stage that contract management, the ongoing process of ensuring that the contract progresses smoothly and in accordance with requirements, begins.

All contracts have risks attached to them. These are aspects of the contract process where things could go wrong. There is a large number of such risks and the contracts officer must try to be aware of them at all times.

Similarly, all contracts have potential rewards and the contracts officer must always be aware of these and be aware of whether they are being achieved by the contract.

There are mechanisms such as the Kraljic matrix can help us to be aware of the risks that may apply to a contract as well as how likely they are to arise and their potential seriousness.

Case Study

Donna Ltd is a large manufacturing company producing a range of very well known machines for the energy market, in the UK and the USA.

It has a turnover of over £100m per annum. Recently it has designed and developed a new generation of high-tech machines, which employs the latest technology and the unique selling proposition of being able to operate using only 30 per cent of the energy consumed by traditional models; it also has a unique control system to reduce the amount of materials needed to achieve excellent results.

One of the key elements is the auto feed control unit, in the industry it is widely known that 95% of all equipment failures and breakdowns can be attributed to faults in this key component. Obviously the contract for this item is fundamental to the success of the product. As the managing director of the company has said in a memo to the production manager, the future of the company is staked on the new product.

Traditionally, the auto feed control unit used in Donna's machines have been obtained from the UK market, in particular Omega Ltd. Jim Peterson, the Contracts Manager, has already suggested that the contract for the auto feed control unit be placed with Omega, a locally-based manufacturing company employing about 100 people. Unemployment in the area is quite high and the current recession has hit the company hard. In recent years Omega has reduced its R&D expenditure and cut back on several major investment programmes. Donna has a corporate strategy, part of which is to support local industry and the local community. The company has sponsored several education and training programmes in conjunction with the local community.

Omega has suffered from quality problems in the past and has had to employ inspectors and checkers to reduce the number of faulty products leaving the factory. Jim Peterson feels sure that with a contract full of clear contractual obligations and improved inspection and checking procedures at Donna's end, he will be able to ensure the consistency of quality. Omega is very competitive on price (up to 10%) a vital factor in the traditional Contracting decision.

Susan French, Director of Contracts, on the other hand, takes a different view. In recent times the improved quality and competitive price of several South Korean suppliers has called the traditional contracting decision into question. One contractor in particular, the SKS Corporation, which has recently established a sales office in London and has a very good reputation in the market place and are well know for their quality.

Jim and Susan have crossed swords on several occasions regarding sourcing decisions. Jim thinks that Susan does not understand the realities of the situation; Omega is a well-known company which has worked closely with Donna. Susan feels that Jim is too conservative and that a more pro-active approach would reap great quality and price rewards. She is determined to use SKS.

At a recent meeting to discuss the issue, the Managing Director had to step in to restore order as Susan and Jim got into a heated debate. Jane Tilly brought them back to earth by pointing out: "The key issue is not whether Omega or SKS are acceptable to us; it's whether they are acceptable to our customers."

This contracting decision is vital to Donna's future. It must be made in the light of that and take into account the cost of having to go through the process again should the decision be less than optimal.

Tasks

Analyse risks and rewards associated with both contractors.

Tendering Methodology

Introduction

One of the most important aspects of contract management is the initial selection of an appropriate contractor to perform the contract. There are two frequently used methods for achieving this which we will examine in this chapter. These are:

• **Open and Closed Tendering** – a formal process whereby contractors are invited from the market place (open) or from a list of re-qualified and approved providers (closed) to submit firm and unequivocal offers.

Many contracts officers use 'open tendering' as a means of selecting the 'right' contractor for any type of contract but when the 'contract' is a major, possibly lengthy, contract, there are some powerful arguments against that process. We will examine some of the considerations around this argument.

Closed Tendering

In order to ensure that only those contractors are invited to bid whose technical capability and management competence are judged adequate for a defined type of work, a specific list of proposed contractors for each tender should be selected from the organisation's approved list if it has one. Much would depend here on the organisation's history of awarding contracts of a similar nature to the one that is in the process of being developed and awarded.

However, an estimated 433-billion Euros (£379-billion) is spent outside procurement departments' approved routes at European companies, according to recent research. Although 95% of organisations have set up preferred contractor lists, just half of the 162 firms surveyed said they had adequate controls to ensure staff who buy use them. On average, there was only 66 per cent compliance to preferred contractor lists and 64 per cent compliance with contracted rates.

It is inadvisable to invite too many contractors to bid for a given contract in view of the considerable costs incurred by contractors in preparing tenders, which will ultimately be reflected in their prices, not to mention the time and effort spent by the buying organisation itself in evaluating the bids. There is no 'ideal' number of potential contractors (tenderers) but many contracts officers would say that three to six is sufficient.

In tendering for major works and services where the local contractor capacity may be limited, it may be advisable to consider inviting bids from international contractors who are not already established in the country. In such cases a specific prequalification exercise should be carried out in order to select a suitable short list of contractors who are technically competent and interested in bidding for the work.

When a project/contract involves complex or new technology it is sometimes advisable to ask a limited number of pre-selected contractors to prepare a feasibility study at a lump sum price, agreed up front, usually based on effort required.

On the basis of these feasibility/optimisation studies, the buying organisation can formulate much more cost effectively the scope of works to be tendered subsequently, and contractors run a much lower risk when submitting bids.

The cost of such pre-tendering feasibility studies should be only a fraction of the overall project costs but, because of the better understanding of the project requirements, could result in significant savings on contracting costs.

Open Tendering

Arguments in favour of open tendering focus on the idea that requesting bids from only a small number of pre-qualified bidders will not stimulate the competitive pressures that should exist in a supply market and that, only by stimulating these pressures will the contracts officer obtain the 'best' deal. The counter-argument is that there is no point in allowing potential contractors who are not capable of completing the contract satisfactorily to submit proposals because, if they are not experienced in the type of work required, they may indulge in 'kite flying'. This would only serve as a waste of the contracts officer's time.

When considering open tendering it should be remembered that public sector organisations and private companies providing public services or utilities (e.g. water companies or railway companies) will be constrained by EU Procurement Directives to use open tendering for contracts that are likely to be above a certain price threshold although there are exceptions. There is the restricted procedure which comprises a two-stage process whereby contractors need to pre-qualify before being allowed to put their bid forward. This procedure is most often employed when there is a need to establish whether or not firms bidding possess the relevant skills or qualifications and would appear to support the perceived advantages of the RFP process detailed above.

It is difficult, if not impossible, to resolve the argument between open tendering and the closed approach but for major, expensive contracts, it would appear that the closed approach has the major advantage of going some way towards ensuring that only contractors that are experienced in and knowledgeable of, the work will be asked to bid. This would go some way towards ensuring that the bid evaluation process should be more straightforward and that time will not be wasted in evaluating bids that originate from potential contractors that would be incapable of performing the contract satisfactorily. Certainly, appraisal of contractors/contractors will be necessary at some stage and carrying it out before the tendering process begins, so that only qualified contractors are requested to provide bids, should provide the advantages mentioned above.

Tendering is potentially a very expensive process. This expense may be justified by the savings and other benefits it may bring to the organisation but there are some potentially major problems with tendering:

Open Tendering and Total Quality Conflicts

The total quality concept suggests that the policies of single sourcing and 'partnership' be adopted so that the contracts officer may work with a chosen contractor over time to improve quality and develop a 'total quality' approach throughout the supply chain. Tendering may be perceived as being in conflict with this aim for the following reasons:

- Emphasis on price as a key variable – the total quality ideal suggests that total cost of ownership is more important than consideration of price alone.

- Need for very tight specification – this goes against the total quality focus on performance specifications

- Emphasis on lowest price, not lowest cost of supply.

- The lowest bidder is accepted so contractor base widens

- The total quality approach tends to lead to a reduction of the supply base.

It is a widely held opinion that the use of Approved Lists can reduce or eliminate these areas of conflict. This is because the evaluation process leading to contractors generally being included in the approved list should focus on quality.

Disadvantages of Open Tendering

- Contractors may quote a price that is too low leading to subsequent disputes if goods or services are unsatisfactory.

- Tendering is unsuitable for certain contracts where consultation with one or more of the more favourable tenderers is often essential in order to clear up some technical points.

- The tendering process is too slow for emergencies.

- Where tenderers are accepted on the principle of the lowest price, credit may not be given to contractors for past performance.

- Tendering can be an expensive procedure for the contracts officer.

- Tendering is expensive for the contractor due to the sometimes complex process of submitting bids.

Technical and Commercial Evaluations (Split Bids)

Normally bids will be jointly evaluated for technical and commercial considerations but in some it may be advisable to separate the technical evaluation from the commercial one. The idea behind split bids is that the user will evaluate the technical offer and will rank them in order of their technical scores. Then the commercial offer is opened by the Contracts Officer.

The contractor who is technically acceptable and offers the lowest price is awarded the contract. This approach, which is popular in some industries (oil and gas) is designed to avoid "gold plating" whereby the user opts for a technical solution that goes beyond what is really fit for purpose and thus increase costs. The main draw back of this approach is that contractors tend to focus on the bear minimum in terms of quality, safety etc. so that they are just compliant and they may work on very small profit margins ands then seek income via the use of minor work orders and variations. The two aspects of bid evaluation are as follows:

Commercial Issues

- Cost and Price (including discounts, price breaks, etc.)

- Quantity – care is required over quantities required on a regular basis such as every week or month.

- Delivery time(s) – again, this is particularly important when repeat deliveries of an item are required by the contracts officer.

- Whether the vendor is offering direct ordering or call-off facility.

- Method and terms of payment – this is always important for any contract although higher value items such as buildings or items of plant and machinery may well have either (or both!) of the following clauses attached to their contract:
  - Retention clause
  - Stage payments

- Duration and terms of any guarantee or warranty – the terms and time period of any guarantees offered by vendors as part of the bidding process may be evaluated and compared as part of that process.

- Maintenance and after-sales costs – these will only apply to contracts of equipment.

- Assembly/installation costs – again, these will only apply to contracts of equipment or buildings.

- Is any price escalation formula envisaged – these have the advantages of being fair to both parties .Accurately monitoring inflation in a manner that is relevant to the specific contract Their only real disadvantage is that they can be unwieldy and time-consuming to monitor.

- Results of life-cycle costing or investment appraisal – this mainly applies to capital items which, by their very nature, are kept by buying organisations for many years and, during this time, the item's 'life-cycle', costs will attach to them. Examples of the kind of costs under consideration are:
  - Cost of spares
  - Cost of maintenance (allied to projected service intervals)

Technical Issues

There is a great amount of variety here in terms of different types of items having different bid evaluation requirements. Bids for branded items will usually be evaluated simply against the variables of price and availability. However, items made especially for the buying organisation (e.g. components used in manufacturing companies) will require full evaluation of these technical aspects.

- **Quality standards** – the importance of evaluating the relative quality of product offered by different contractors cannot be overstated.

- **The extent to which the product matches the specification** – for items that are likely to have a fundamental effect on the operation of the contracts officer's company's finished product or have a critical supporting role of some sort it is vital that specifications are carefully considered, as follows:

- Specifications lower than requested; these might, upon consideration, be accepted and might give the contracts officer a lower price and/or better availability. This kind of evaluation must be made by technical personnel.
- Specifications higher than requested; these might be accepted because they might be able to improve the contracts officer's company's product or service such as to provide competitive advantage although this may mean higher prices.

The quality and appropriateness of the specification will go a long way towards determining how successful the item is and will have a major effect on input costs.

- Test results – it may well be worth having samples of items tested before a decision to contract is made.

- Variation from specification – this refers to situations where contractors, in effect, say "we cannot supply exactly what we want but we can supply this item that we believe will satisfy their requirements". The usual contracts officer's reaction would be to ignore such a bid but it could be worth investigating.

- Availability period for spares – for many capital items, this can be critical.

- Terms and conditions of contract.

A good system for analysing/evaluating quotations is to use a scorecard or bid tabulation, in the form of a grid or matrix shown below:

	Contractor	A	B	C
Selection criteria				
Price				
Delivery period				
Quality				
Etc.				

This bid tabulation allows we to see at a glance how potential sources compare.

Appraisal of Contractors

Appraisal of contractors should follow a well-defined process such as is described below and selection of the 'right' contractor will include consideration of the well-known Ray Carters 9 C's model for contractor selection. Having an effective selection process, weighting systems, validity and evidence is critical to the process. The validity of the evidence submitted by the contractor needs to be verified. This is measured in the model by reviewing and assessing the information provided against the following key statements:

Statement	Factor
Evidence is complete, verified, current, comprehensive, observed, measured, provided by third party, independent	4
Almost complete, verified, some observation, contribution of desk research and observation. Some use of past records	3
Reliance on past records, lack of observation, totally based upon desk research, not complete, some verification	2

The validity or quality of the evidence is scored and is then reflected in the overall score awarded to the contractor.

Critical Selection Criteria for Contractors

The extent and rigour with which the well-known 9Cs process is applied is dependent upon a number of factors, including:

- Contract risk.

- Contract spend.

- Criticality of contract outcome.

- Complexity of work required to complete the contract successfully.

The higher the total values of these variables, the greater should be the extent and rigour of the appraisal process. The 9Cs process is as follows:

- **Competence**
    - This is the ability of the contractor to perform the contract.

- **Capacity**
  'To meet present and future demands': if the contractor does not have sufficient capacity, the timely completion of the contract is unlikely. Evidence of such capacity might be as follows:
  - Order book – what is the state of the contractor's order book?
  - Forecasts – what future business does the contractor forecast that it is likely to obtain?
  - Administrative resources – Does the contractor have the necessary systems and procedures to support good quality and service?

- **Consistency**
  This is the contractor's ability to provide consistent levels of quality and services. Evidence of this would arise from:
  - Contractor's reputation
  - Outputs – the buying organisation's Quality Manager should inspect a sample of the contractor's work output to ascertain product quality at first hand.
  - History – it is useful for the contracts officer to request references relating to other customers from the contractor.

- **Control of Key Processes**
  It is important to try to gain a 'feel' for how the contractor manages and controls these 'key' processes. Each is important, in its own way, in terms of ensuring that they are able to supply the goods in line with the 5 'rights' of procurement. Examples of how each of these might contribute to the achievement of the '5 rights' might include:
  - Inventory – if the contractor carries enough stock they are likely to be able to supply the right quantity

at the right time although carrying too much stock will adversely affect their ability to supply at the right price because of excessive input costs.

- Quality – control of the contractor's quality processes enables them to supply at the right quality.
- Operations – good control of operations will enable the contractor to supply at the right time and in the right quantity and will have an effect on the right quality.
- Procurement – companies are heavily dependent on key contractors to provide good quality, service, innovation, etc., while keeping costs down.
- Marketing and to a greater extent, distribution – good, efficient processes here will allow the contractor to supply at the right time and in the right quantity.
- HSE – good systems and procedures here, such as a good safety record will contribute to the morale and motivation of the contractor's workforce.

- **Cost**
  A full analysis should be carried out to examine the following:
  - Profit – is the contractor profitable?
  - Variable costs – costs directly associated with production and which increase with production volume.
  - Fixed costs – The contracts officer should assess and analyse the specific level of such contribution.
  - Margins – what is the contractor's profit margin
  - Break-even point – this is the quantity of production where total costs equal revenue. Above this point the contractor makes a profit and below this, a loss.

- **Commitment to Quality**
  Does the contractor have a quality policy and a commitment to its success? This may be assessed by examination of

whether the contractor used any or all of the following.

- SPC – Statistical Process Control
- TQM – Total Quality Management.
- QC – Quality Control – what specific measures does the contractor employ to measure the quality of output?
- CIP – Constant Improvement Processes.
- Culture and values – does the contractor have an organisational culture and a set of corporate values, communicated to everyone who works there, which focus on quality and its achievement/improvement at all times?
- ISO 9001/14001 – is the contractor accredited to either of these standards?

- **Clean**
  Contractors and their products/services should satisfy legislative and other environmental requirements such as ISO 14001.

- **Culture and Relationships**
  Contractors and client should share similar values.

- **Cash/Finance**
  It is important that any contractor has 'financial stability' and evidence of this might be taken from:
  - Balance sheet
  - Profit and loss account
  - Credit rating
  - Reputation – what kind of reputation for, e.g. financial propriety or profitability, does the contractor have?

- **Communication**
  - Although it may seem obvious, contractors need to be asked how they will communicate with the client. Will it be by fax, email or telephone? Communication

also covers the ICT software and applications that the supplier has. If they only have very basic ICT facilities, they will be unable to communicate effectively.

Contract Execution/Completion

Once the highest scoring contractor has been selected and the contract awarded, its progress must be monitored and managed up to its conclusion. The selection of an effective contractor is by no means the end of the process and is, in fact, only a small part. This will be dealt with in some depth in other parts of this book, notably in chapters 6, 9 and 14.

Chapter summary

In this chapter we have considered the means of tendering, both 'closed' and 'open' that are widely used in procurement. Both methods have advantages and disadvantages but the closed method can be seen to have some advantages over the open method when we are dealing with complex, potentially long-lasting, contracts.

We have also considered the appraisal of potential contractors that often takes place prior to the approved/closed process in order to ensure that only suitable contractors submit bids.

Case Study

The Pharmaceutical Agency is a wholly owned government organisation, set up to manage and administer the collection of royalty payments from drug companies operating within the UK. The Agency is about to embark upon a complete upgrade of its payments system. This will involve integrating from a well established (but traditional) clerical based system to a fully integrated IT based system.

The key customers of this new system include the CEO, plus Finance and Operations, both headed by strong personalities who have already started to have "initial" discussions with several of the approved major IT providers in the market place.

The Agency is under pressure to demonstrate its added value and the need to make things happen quickly and effectively. The Head of Finance states "we need to get this project off the ground as soon as possible; we should use the scope of work provided by our approved providers in the market place. They have experience of implementing similar systems and we could start the process of closed tendering immediately".

The Head of the Agencies legal section has highlighted the fact that given the value of this project, the contract must go through the full rigour of the EU "Open" contracting process. She states "this will no doubt frustrate the customer, alienate the contractors, but it has to be done and we have no choice in the matter".

The Head of Operations is keen to get the project up and running, but he favours extending the scope of the existing IT support contract, currently with Delta Consultants. This is a medium sized organisation, specialising in providing IT consultants support to the public sector. The company has a standard consultancy contract with Delta. The Head of Operations states "why go through the whole "open" or indeed the "closed" tender process when we think we already have an adequate contractor in place?".

Task

As a consultant what advice would you give to the Agency's CEO?

5 Types of Contract

Introduction

There are many occasions where the wrong type of pricing model used on a contract can lead to an unsatisfactory outcome. As an extreme example, Lord Fraser, in the Holyrood Inquiry concerning the construction of the Scottish Parliament, stated quite unequivocally:

> *"I regard the decision to adopt construction management without advising Ministers of the attendant risks and the inflexible insistence on a rigid programme as among the most flawed decisions in the history of the Project."*

In addition in giving evidence, Colin Carter of Gardiner & Theobald, providers of independent professional advice and services to the property and construction sectors stated: "If we are a client who is dependent on having a fixed price before we start, we do not choose to go construction management, because it does not deliver that." – *Holyrood Inquiry, Chapter 6, Construction Management.*

This chapter looks at the different types of contract and their advantages and disadvantages, followed by a similar analysis of pricing models.

Types of Contract

There are many different types of contract, often with subtle differences, but normally reflecting the degree of control, by either the customer or the contractor.

A turnkey contract is an arrangement in which requirements are in a completed state, where a single contractor manages the entire contract from start to finish without customer input. Thus the contractor is carrying out contract and "handing the key" over to the customer who turns it on. In this particular instance, a single contractor will be responsible, not only for his own output, but for managing all the works carried out by other contractors. For example, in the case of contract for a new warehouse, the customer would let a contract to a single turnkey contractor, who would in turn let sub-contracts to such disciplines such as heating and ventilation, electrical installations, mechanical plant such as hoists and storage racking. This has several advantages for the customer in that:

- Contract administration is reduced. The customer has to manage only one contractor, who bears the risk and responsibility for managing all other contractors.

- The contractor is motivated to complete the job as he fully bears the risk of late completion.

- The customer only takes over the works, when they are complete to his satisfaction.

- The contractor is likely to have more experience in managing high value, high risk contracts of this type, particularly in the civil and building construction disciplines.

However the customer may find that:

- There is a lack of control over design, sourcing and construction decisions.

- The cost of management of the contract by the contractor is built into the final price in the form of an overhead.

- He is tempted to interfere with the management of the contract adding to his own administration costs and potentially bearing some of the risks that should reside with the contractor.

- He is so dependent on a single contractor, that it is difficult or impossible to change, should this contractor underperform or be in breach of contract.

- There is a limited number of contractors able to carry out this type of contract.

The opposite to this type of contract is a client-coordinated (or traditional approach). Instead of a single contractor managing the scope of the works including all of the sub-contractors, the customer breaks the scope into individual packages of work and manages them all separately. Using the warehouse example given above, the customer would let and manage each of contracts himself.

The advantages are:
- The customer maintains maximum direct control of all of the contractors, rather than being one step removed from them as sub-contractors.

- This approach allows for separation of design and construction, taking advantage of using different contractors for differing skills as well as allowing for competition on the construction element against an independently produced design.

- The customer may feel that he has a greater direct control over health, safety and environmental issues.

- The overhead cost of paying the contractor to manage is avoided.

However, the customer has to bear:
- The cost of managing a large number of contractors, either as an internal cost if his own staff are used or, as is common, the cost of employing an external project management consultant to carry this out.

- A significant degree of risk in the event of under-performance by any of the contractors. For example, if the heating and ventilation contractor is late and this affects the overall completion of the warehouse, then the customer bears the responsibility and potential extension of time costs payable to the main building contractor.

- The risk of any failures in the design, for which the contractor may have little or no input.

It is also possible to employ a partial turnkey approach, where the main contractor manages some of the work packages and the customer some of the others. This is a mixture of the turnkey and client-coordinated types of contract and would be subject to the advantages and disadvantages of both of these approaches.

Other types of contracting model include the following:

In the case of **Management Contracting**, the customer appoints a contractor, who acts in a project management role by managing all of the sub-contractors, but unlike Turnkey Contracting does not carry out any of the work himself. The management contractor is paid a fee (fixed or percentage) for carrying out this role. This has an additional advantage to Turnkey Contracting in that the Management Contractor retains a degree of independence from the actual construction process, though the customer may feel that he is several steps removed from the actual works.

The contracting type described in the introduction as **Construction Management** is on the face of it similar to Management Contracting, but in this case, the client retains the direct contractual link with each of the contactors, but appoints a Construction Manager to manage the works. This is often used (and notoriously so in the case of the Scottish Parliament) as a fast track strategy, for letting individual packages of work, before design is complete. Though this has the advantage of speeding up the process, the customer has no certainty of the final cost until completion and thus is bearing any risk of cost overrun.

The final model that we shall examine is **Private Finance Initiative (PFI)** contracts. This was introduced in the 1990s and employs a completely different philosophy, whereby the contractor designs, finances, builds and operates (DFBO) a building, road and service under a concession from a Public Sector customer and earns a profit through charges paid to him during a specified lifetime of the asset. The key features are:

- The Public Sector retains the role as main purchaser or the essential enabler, but does not own the asset.

- The Private sector contractor arranges the finance for the contract, usually by setting up a Special Purpose Vehicle (SPV), which acts the contracting entity with financing in the form of equity from the contractor (or contractors, if it is a joint venture) and financial institutions and loans from banks etc.

- Ownership may be transferred in future (possibly 25 to 30 years) depending on what is specified in the contract.

- The risk is transferred to the contractor, who recovers costs and earns profit from two main types of arrangement as follows:

- Freestanding – where the contractor's costs are recovered through charges to final user such as the M6 Toll road near Birmingham.

- Services sold to public sector – where the contractor's costs are recovered directly through a charge to a public body (known as a unitary charge), but the service is free to the end user such as Queen Elizabeth Hospital in London.

The advantages of PFI to the customer and ultimately the taxpayer are:

- There is no capital outlay for the public sector as the capital expenditure is entirely financed by the private sector. This also releases capital funds for other projects or allows projects to go ahead, which might never happen.

- There is reduced risk to the Public Sector.

- Contractors' expertise in project management, design, build and operation can be exploited.

- Payments are only made to the contractor, once the service is being provided.

- Budgeting is assisted as costs are known in the case of the unitary charge or paid by the end user for a Freestanding PFI.

The disadvantages of PFI are:

- It is costly to manage the tender and contract administration processes.

- There are only a limited number of companies able to handle such arrangements.

- As contractors are paid over a long period, they may over-recover and ultimately the long-term cost to the tax-payer may be greater, than through use of a conventional procurement route.

- Where a PFI Contractor is consistently under-performing, it may be difficult to remove him and quickly find an alternative.

Contract Pricing Models

Introduction

The form of pricing employed within the contract ultimately determines allocation of risk. It is an important that risk is borne by the party, who is in the best position to manage it. This ability will normally be dictated by the following:

- Where the organisation sits on the "risk continuum". The public sector is less likely to want to bear contractual risk, than say a venture capitalist or entrepreneur.

- The nature of the relationship between the parties, be they wishing to transfer risk or whether there is a willingness to share risk.

- The certainty with which the scope of work or specification can be defined.

- The likelihood of changes to the scope of work, whether planned or unplanned.

Pricing Models

A Lump Sum/Firm Price is perhaps the simplest model, where a contract with a reasonably well-defined scope of works is let, for which a known price is agreed within the contract, risks are reasonably well defined and is only varied where the scope is changed by agreement of both parties. This is advantageous to the customer in that:

- The risk is firmly with the contractor in that any failure by him to correctly estimate or manage his costs will be his responsibility with no recourse for additional money from the customer.

- Because the contractor is motivated to manage costs, the requirement for supervision of effort expended by the customer will be minimal. Any delays he incurs will be at his own expense.

- Such a pricing method gives a high degree of certainty for budgeting purposes.

However:

- The contractor may include contingency in the quoted price in order to cover the possibility of inaccurate estimation or unexpected cost increases.

- Where a firm price has been requested from the contractor for a poorly defined scope, he may once again include contingency and he may also be more likely to submit requests for variations and claims (See Chapter 9).

- The contractor may seek to cut corners on quality in order to reduce cost/ increase his profit.

A variation on the above might be a **Fixed Price with a variation clause**, which builds into the contract the opportunity at defined intervals to vary the price in accordance with an agreed price variation formula, using a mechanism such as the Consumer Price Index (CPI). This has the advantage that the contractor does not have to build inflation into the contingency, but also means that the customer no longer has price certainty.

An alternative is to use a **Schedule of Rates**, which can be described as a "shopping list" or "cart" of unit rates for either goods or services, which are able to be reasonably clearly specified. This can be used where the type of good or service is required is known, but not the quantity. These can often be seen on a construction contract, where the materials, services required can only be estimated and put together in the form of a Bill of Quantities. Using the construction of the stores as an example, it will be known that concrete will require to be poured for the foundations, but not necessarily how much, depending on ground conditions, so the tenderer is asked to price per cubic meter against an estimated quantity.

A similar use of Schedule of Rates might be for a framework contract for a range of services that may or may not be required over a given period. For example there may be a rate for servicing a pump including all labour, materials, travel and overheads, but once again the customer may not know how often this is required. The advantages of this type of pricing are:

- The customer can enter into a contractual relationship without knowing exact quantities at the time of tendering.

- The contractor still bears the risk of underestimating or unexpected cost increases in respect of the rates quoted. In the above example, he will receive a firm price for servicing the pump, irrespective of any changes in cost or in the time taken to carry out the work.

- Where new requirements occur, additional rates can be easily added to the contract.

- Useful pricing information is available for estimating any future costs.

However:

- Where a bill of quantities is used, the tenderer may overprice items that he thinks have been underestimated in the Bill of Quantities, in order to gain an advantage in any tender assessment.
- The customer no longer has cost certainty.

- The contract management and supervision resource (such as Quantity Surveyors) is greater than for a fixed price.

Where there is uncertainty about the overall scope of contract (e.g. for Research and Development or unknown fault repair), it is often appropriate to use a **Cost Reimbursable** type contract. There are many variations to these, but the two main types are **Cost-Plus** and **Time and Materials**.

In the case of Cost-Plus, the contractor is paid on the basis of costs incurred with either a fixed fee or a percentage of the costs incurred as profit. Time and Materials is not too dissimilar except that the payment is made on the basis of an agreed daily or hourly rate which will also cover overheads and profit. Materials and plant hire will also be charged at cost plus an agreed overhead. These are particularly useful means of contracting, where the scope of work is difficult to define, as the tenderer will not need to add contingency to the price in order to cover any such uncertainties.

However, such an approach is fraught with difficulties because:

- There is no incentive for the contractor to minimise costs. In fact the longer the works last and the more inefficient he is, the higher the profit.

- A high degree of supervision is required to ensure that the contractor works efficiently.

- It may be difficult to establish what costs can be reasonably charged such as the cost of re-work.

A degree of trust is required between both customer and contractor, otherwise dubious practices may occur such as:

- Double charging where certain costs may appear in the overheads, as well as a separate cost, such as some types of Head Office staff, computing time.

- The same contractor is carrying out Cost Reimbursable and Firm Price work side by side, leading to the claiming of staff costs under the cost reimbursable contract at the same time as work is being carried out under a Firm Price contract.

- Unnecessarily early delivery of plant to gain additional revenue on hire charges.

- Charging for non-existent labour or materials.

To mitigate some of the issues that might arise with Cost Reimbursable Contracts, it may be appropriate to use a **Target Cost Incentive Fee (TCIF)** arrangement. In these types of contract a target cost (including an agreed profit) is negotiated between the customer and contractor, based on detailed analysis of what is a reasonable target, through probability or sensitivity analysis.

Where the final outturn cost is less than the target, then the customer and contractor share the savings (known as "gainshare"). Conversely any cost overruns (i.e. greater than the target) are also shared (known as "painshare").

Such arrangements will incentivise the contractor to minimise the final outturn price and provide on break on the escalation of costs. However such a contract should not be entered into lightly because:

- It is very difficult to agree the target. The contractor would like this to be high, whilst the customer wishes it to be more "stretching".

- It is very resource intensive to manage.

- Changes in the outline scope or objectives or the imposition of unavoidable external costs may cause the contractor to put pressure on the customer to increase the target.

An independent review will investigate whether pricing rules for single supplier UK defence contracts should be changed to get better value for money. Lord Currie will lead the review of single source procurement – where only one defence supplier is invited to tender The review will examine the framework for pricing work to be procured under single source conditions and consider whether costs can be reduced and efficiency increased.

Chapter Summary

In this chapter, we have examined different types of contracting and pricing models. The use of these will depend on the willingness to bear or transfer risk and the degree to how well the scope of work is defined. We have examined the following types of contract:

- Turnkey

- Client-coordinated

- Partial Turnkey

- Management Contracting

- Construction Management

- Private Finance Initiative

We have also examined the following pricing methods:

- Firm Price/Lump Sum

- Fixed Price with a variation clause

- Schedule of Rates

- Cost Reimbursable including Cost-Plus and Time and Materials

- Target Cost Incentive Fee (TCIF).

Case Study

Morris, the Head of Safety and Environment at Emirates Engineering is becoming more and more concerned about the poor state of the local pumping station and the risk of a major accident and personal injury is steadily increasing. The pump house is due for major refurbishment. He feels obliged to send a memo (below) to the Engineering Manager and Maintenance Manager expressing his concerns.

In response to this, the Maintenance Manager verbally instructs Delta Contractors, a local contracting company, to commence work at once. He decides to utilise a series of Time and Materials type contracts designed for small miscellaneous civil works. Company policy is for all works to go to tender, even those under $50,000 and should be let on the basis of the lowest price.

MEMO
To: Maintenance Manager and Engineering Manager
From: HSE Manager

Accident Risk in the Pump House – The poor state of the floor in the pump house is creating an unacceptable level of risk re personal injury. I must ask we to deal with this issue as a matter of urgency. – *HSE Manager*

The terms of Time and Materials contracts are quite harsh on the contractor and the Maintenance Manager feels well satisfied that all the "risks" have been passed to the contractor, even though he is not sure what the risks actually are in the case of the $2m pump house refurbishment project. Delta view these terms as unfair, but have accepted this verbal instruction on the basis of their commercial strategy This involves gaining the contract and then seeking variations by exploiting unclear specification and poor scopes of work. Delta have financial problems, due to recent cut backs by other clients and they desperately need the work.

The Engineering Manager and the Maintenance Manager have both tried to minimise the involvement of the Supply Chain Management Division, both feel they will only hold up the programme and that the whole project will get bogged down in bureaucracy. They know that the SCMD will insist that the work should go to competitive tender and be submitted to the major tender board for approval

Within a few weeks of the works commencing problems start to occur. The Contractor is unsure of what is required and is constantly seeking advice and guidance from both the Engineering Manager and the Maintenance Manager. Both are very busy and tend to delegate this to the Contract Administrator. When they do provide instructions there are normally "contradictory". The contract administrator is responsible for the overall monitoring of the project, but has no real scope of work or performance metrics, given the lack of formal instructions. He is also finding it difficult to convince Finance to make payments for work done re "major repairs and refurbishment" against a series of Time and Materials contracts that have a maximum value of $50,000 per transaction. The Contractor has also been in contact with the local site manager with regard to late payment of invoices. So far the total cost of the work completed is $1m and the work is only just started.

Task

What are the problems and what are the solutions?

6 Contract Administration

Introduction

This chapter looks specifically at contract administration, which may be thought of as the role which is carried out after the contract has been awarded, with the key objective of ensuring that the requirements of the contract have been achieved, in terms of a safe outcome to time, cost and quality. This can be differentiated from contract management, which covers those activities which aim to obtain added value from the contract, through supplier relationship management, innovation and cost reduction. Though some of the following applies to contracts for the supply of goods, in the main, the descriptions will be aimed at service and works contracts.

A good example of this is the billions of dollars have been wasted by the US government's poor use of contractors in Iraq and Afghanistan. The USA Commission on Wartime Contracting has said in a recent interim report. The commission, a bipartisan group that studies wartime contracts, concluded that the US has wasted tens of billions of the $177 billion (£109 billion) it has spent on deals and grants to support the military, reconstruction and other US operations in Iraq and Afghanistan since 2001.

Inaugural Meeting

After the contract has been awarded, one of the first key contract administration requirements is to hold the Inaugural Meeting (also known as the kick-off or start-up meeting). This is generally one of the first face-to-face meetings between the customer and the newly appointed contractor. It is important to be clear:

- What the purpose of such a meeting is.

- Who should be present?

- What should be discussed?

- What should not be discussed?

The purpose of the meeting may include the following objectives:

- To introduce the customer's and contractor's key personnel.

- To ensure key objectives are clearly understood.

- To communicate who has authority on each side to carry out specific requirements under the contract. For example, the contract manager may inform the contractor's representative that he delegates certain powers under the contract to nominated staff, such as certifying completion of work, issuing of variations or settling claims up to a defined value.

- To ensure both sides are aware of the standards required, particularly on health, safety, environment and quality.

- To ensure the contractor's readiness for setting to work.

- To emphasise any key issues or risks that might arise from the contract.

- To establish how the relationship will work in practice.

The contract manager and the contractor's representative (their site manager or their project manager for example) should as a minimum be present. On the customer's side, the following may also be present by invitation, to all or only the relevant parts of the meeting:

- The procurement officer.

- Technical experts.

- The project manager.

- Health, safety and environment specialists.

The contractor's site or project manager may also include such persons as the design, construction and commissioning managers.

There is no standard agenda; it is important that it is tailored to the specific issues relevant to the contract. Some potential items include the following:

- Routes and addresses for correspondence, such as document submission, letters, variations, claims, approval of sub-contractors.

- Procedures for certifying work.

- Management of technical documentation such as:
  - Permits for work
  - Design submissions
  - Drawings
  - Method Statements
  - Operation and maintenance manuals.

- Management of the contract programme.

- Reporting requirements.

- Security.

- Health, safety and environment issues.

- Quality requirements and non-conformances.

- Invoicing Procedure.

The inaugural meeting should not be used for the following:
- Negotiating outstanding contractual issues, that had not been able to be agreed at contract award.

- Discussion or approval of variations to the scope of work.

- A means for one party to try to gain an initial advantage over the other.

Induction and Site Familiarisation

The inaugural meeting is concerned with familiarising the contractor's management team with the customer's personnel and methods and standards of working. When site work commences, it is important that the contractor's staff and sub-contractors are also aware of the key issues when working on the customer's site. This will normally be achieved through carrying out an induction process, where a member of the customer's staff will hold a training session covering topics such as the following:
- Health, safety and environment policies, procedures and standards including:
  - Key hazards.
  - Accident and near miss reporting.
  - First aid.
  - Occupational health.
  - Housekeeping.

- Security procedures including restricted areas.

- Location of facilities, such as the canteen, toilets, welfare facilities.

- Behavioural standards.

This may be followed by a written examination test to ensure understanding of the key requirements and then by a site familiarisation, where contractor's staff are shown the key work areas and any issues or hazards specific to that particular work area.

Approval of Designs and Drawings

Where the contractor is responsible for an element of design in the contract, it is important that approval processes are fully specified in the contract and that these are fully complied with whilst the contract is running. There are some key issues with this process:

- The conditions of contract should be absolutely clear that any approval by the customer of such submissions does not in way remove any obligations of the contractor in respect of the quality or fitness for purpose of the design or drawing submission.

- Submissions by the contractor should be in writing as should the customer's acceptance or rejection. Adequate time for this process should be allowed for either explicitly in the contract or by agreement at each submission.

- Where the submission is rejected, it is important that reasons are given, which must refer either to failure to meet the agreed specification or a specific condition of contract. If a concession is granted by the customer to allow such a rejection to pass, this should then be issued as variation, with any consequent price reduction agreed.

Contract Programme

For a contract, which has specific detailed deliverables at its conclusion, there will normally be need for a contract programme. Unless the requirement is simple and short-term, it will not normally be sufficient to rely solely upon purely monitoring the completion or delivery date. The customer will want to gain assurance that the contractor is carrying out the services or works in a manner that does not prejudice completion on time.

A tool that is used to achieve is a contract programme, where the contractor details the following:

- Key activities including their length, sequence and dependency on other activities.

- Key milestones.

- Resourcing requirements, such as quantities of labour, key materials and plant.

- The critical path or the minimum time that must be allowed in order to meet the completion date.

In order to ensure that contractor is carrying out the work in accordance with the programme, progress meetings may be used as a means of monitoring and agreeing how any deviations from the programme may be agreed.

These meetings must be minuted and the contents formally agreed. The frequency of these meetings will depend on the length and complexity of the project.

Risk Registers

A Risk Register (sometimes known as Risk Log) is a tool used for identifying, analysing, mitigating, monitoring and ultimately closing off risks. They are often used at company, department, project or contract level. In the latter case, they are often shared and jointly owned by the customer and contractor on high value complex projects.

A typical risk register might include:

- Details of the actual risk.

- The risk owner with the responsibility for managing and trying to mitigate the risk.

- The probability of the risk coming to fruition. This is often expressed as a numerical figure, with the higher the value, the greater likelihood of an occurrence.

- Impact. This is often expressed as a numerical figure, with the higher the value, the greater the consequence.

- Action. What measures are being put in place to mitigate the risk?

- Cost. How much will these measures cost?

Certification of Work

In order for the contractor to receive payment, it is necessary have a process to indicate that the contractor's obligations have been fulfilled.

For the supply of goods, this may be little more than a signed Goods Received Note or for a low value, short term service, an endorsing of a supplier's invoice by the customer that an the requirements has been completed in accordance with contract and that the invoice can now be paid.

For longer-term, higher value contracts, receiving payment at the end of the contract will probably not be a viable option. For contractors to be able to perform a contract adequately, they need to be able to finance labour costs, purchases of materials and hire of plant. Therefore many contracts have defined processes for work certification at intervals during the contract, through various forms of stage payments, based on the quantity of work completed. These include:

- Interim Payments – made on a regular basis, normally monthly.

- Progress Payments – made on the basis of the percentage of work completed, such as 25, 50 or 75%

- Milestone Payments – made on the basis of completion of work up to defined key points or milestones in the contracts, such as completion of design or manufacture.

- Advance payments – made in advance of the work being completed, often used by contractors to secure supplies of materials early in the contract, but unpopular with customers, as monies are being paid out with no work completed to show for it.

In addition some contracts may specify a **retention**, whereby an agreed figure is deducted from the value of work certified for payment (often 10% of the contract value). This is withheld until completion, when say half (i.e. 5%) will be released to the contractor with the other half (i.e. 5% again), released at the end of the Defects Period. The purpose of this is to give the contractor an incentive to correct any defects that might occur, by holding back a sum of money. This is less popular with contractors, who do not like having to wait longer to receive a portion of their entitlement to payment and they may price the job at tender stage to take account of this inconvenience.

Health, Safety and Environment

The customer must ensure that legal requirements for health, safety and environment are complied with (see Chapter 10). This section describes the various tools that the customer can use or ensure that the contractor uses to minimise the possibility of harm to persons, plant or the environment.

- **Tool-box talks** – where the contractor's site manager or supervisor assembles the work force on a regular basis (say weekly) to give a talk or presentation on specific health or safety topics, which may be pertinent to the work that this being carried out (e.g. confined space procedures for staff working underground). It is also recommended the contract manager attend these meetings, as he can gain assurance from the key messages being put across as well as showing the contractor, that he is vigilant on health, safety and environmental issues.

- **Safety inspections and audits** – the contract manager may carry out regular or unannounced inspections, possibly accompanied by a member of the contractor's staff. There is also an expectation that the contractor would carry out his own inspections and discuss the results and any relevant actions with the contract manager. Topics could include such matters as use of personal protective equipment, safety of scaffolding, signage etc.

- **Risk assessments** – For any task that a contractor is going to carry out, we would expect to see a health, safety (and environmental) written risk assessment. This would be carried out in the same manner as any other type of risk assessment i.e. the contractor should assess the probability and impact of any identified risk, except that the consequences of such a risk becoming reality are potential death, injury, damage or harm to the environment.

- **Method statements** – These are documents produced by the contractor which provides detailed instructions to staff or sub-contractors on how to perform specific tasks in a manner which will achieve the level of quality required by the contractor minimising risk to health, safety and the environment. They will therefore identify specific steps required in the job, the skills and or qualifications of the person carrying out the operation and refer to any control measures that are required to be taken. For example, an operation which required grinding the sharp edges of a piece of metal might specify a requirement for eye and hand protection or refer to a procedure detailing such a requirement. Other requirements for other tasks might include isolation from the electric supply, barriers to prevent to falling, controlled access etc.

- **Reviewing competence** – The contract manager needs to have the assurance that any staff or sub-contractors working for the contractor have the necessary competence to carry out their designated tasks. Although this is ultimately the contractor's responsibility, there are potential quality and safety consequences, if staff are carrying out task beyond their competence. There are several methods of checking staff competence.
  - Checking CVs and training records.
  - Observing the levels of supervision.
  - Observing individuals at the point of work.
  - Discussing the task with individual to assess whether:

- They have received adequate training.
- Whether they have had suitable instructions and method statements.
- They understand any inherent safety risks in carrying out their tasks.

Record Keeping

As a general principle it is important to keep, good detailed records as they give necessary information to:

- To facilitate good contract management through use of reliable data.

- Give an accurate picture of the progress of the contract to other key stakeholders such as regulators, customers.

- To be used as evidence in a dispute with the contractor, where he may have a different interpretation of the event.

- Provide a satisfactory audit trail.

- Provide evidence of work completed.

There are many types of records that may need to be kept such as:

- A daily diary or contract log including such details as:
  - Labour on site.
  - Materials delivered.
  - Plant on site.
  - Accidents or near misses.
  - Delays or waiting time.
  - Weather conditions.
  - Issues raised by either party, including discussions, decisions taken, actions agreed.

- Photographs, audio or video recordings.
- Meeting minutes.
- Commercial information such as variations and claims.
- General Correspondence.

Electronic Contract Management and Administration Systems

There is a growing trend toward the use of electronic and web based contract management and administrative systems. These services have the ability to reduce the administrative costs of managing and letting contracts. These include:

- **E Tendering** – from simple quotes to full tenders the e-tendering process gives control and visibility to the contracting process. Clarifications are easily dealt with ensuring that every tenderer receives the information. Electronic documents with score sheets can be created to facilitate the evaluation of large number of returns during the tendering process.

- **E Contract Management** – these can be fully integrated with e-tendering systems. The contract management process provides the contract register with no limit to the amount of information recorded. Access to contract information including documents can be controlled and where this is relevant published to the pubic area of the web site facilitating request made under the Freedom of Information Act. Included in the process is KPI functionality to allow contract managers to measure the contracted supplier performance against the agreed service levels. Warning flags can be set when performance drops below the agreed service level.

- **E Auctions** – this gives contracting the opportunity to set up an on line auction, at the end of the tendering process to allow selected contractors to bid for the goods or services helping to further reduce costs and achieve value for money. The process manages auctions with multiple items and can include non-price criteria during the bidding process

- **E Contractor Management** – contractors maintain their own information file and the system will prompt contractors and procurement managers when supplier documentation is going out of date. Contractors can then upload for example their latest accounts and insurance documentation from their secure area of the web portal. Warning flags can automatically appear against a supplier record when a document goes out of date and user defined workflows can be created to monitor supplier documentation once it has been uploaded. When a supplier record is changed the system takes a snapshot of the data for auditing purposes. Supplier Management functionality is part of the tendering and contract management process.

- **E Report Writer** – User friendly wizard; the contracts officer can simply select from a list of database fields and then select which fields they want to filter to create and store reports for future use and interrogation.

As well as saving money and time, these processes ensures compliance with the essential elements of governmental sourcing guidelines for public sector procurement, including: Privacy, Authenticity, Integrity and Non-repudiation.

Chapter Summary

This chapter has described some of the matters to be considered, when administering a contract. Good contract administration in itself will not guarantee a successful outcome, but bad contract administration will almost certainly lead to a failure.

Case Study

High Power Case Study – Contract administration

The High Power Oil and Gas company is a well-established sub surface equipment company, based in Dubai. Recently the company let and signed a contract for the refurbishment of its canteen facilities on all its major sites. The outline scope of work was given to the contractor by the Catering manager. Within a few months of the works commencing, the Contract Administrator for this contract is taken ill and is expected to be on sick leave for several months.

His replacement cannot locate the contract file or the contract execution plan that relates to the current work being undertaken. The Contractor has requested payment in advance for the next stage of the project and insists that this was agreed with the original Administrator and a "file" note was made to that effect. The new Administrator is very unhappy with the aggressive attitude of the contractor and his demands for a number of "variations" to the original instructions, albeit verbal ones given by the absent Administrator. The Contractor states:

"We undertook to refurbish the canteen facilities, not rebuild them! which is what your Catering Manager seems to want now? I insist that the variations I have requested are granted, otherwise we stop work!"

The Administrator realises that some of the work is only half completed and a walk out by the Contractor will delay the opening of the canteen for several weeks if not months. He is also conscious that the next phase of a major project is planned for a few months' time and availability of the canteen is critical to its successful performance. The local staff representative has got to hear of this possible delay and makes it known it could develop into a staff welfare issue, given that poor condition of the canteen and that staff are not being properly feed and therefore the company is in breach of contract. The Contractor is still demanding variations and advance payment, while the Manager refuses to even meet to discuss the issue. The Contract Administrator hopes that his "adversial" posture will intimidate the Contractor into withdrawing his claims – he is banking on the contractor not wanting to walk off the job and risk losing the rest of the contract. The Contractor on the other hand cannot undertake the work required (and indeed) demanded by the Catering Manager at the price originally quoted. He will have no choice but to withdraw.

At a recent Senior Management Team meeting the issue of the canteen contract work is raised. The Contracts Manager is asked to provide details of the works to date and the minutes from the contract monitoring and control meeting, which is meant to take place on a regular basis between the company and contractor representatives. "Unfortunately," he states, "I am unable to find the minutes, as you know the last Administrator is on sick leave".

Later that day he calls the current Administrator to see if he knows where the minutes are and also for a copy of the contract diary log. He is unable to provide any information. The Contracts Manager is forced to ask the contractor if he has any information regarding the minutes or log book.

The Contractor realises the Contracts Manager is having difficulties with his senior stakeholders and agrees to provide copies of his "notes" in return for immediate agreement to the first round of variations and the payment of all outstanding invoices. The Contracts Manager is very unhappy, but agrees. The Contractor insists that this be put into writing and emailed forthwith.

TASK

What are the root causes of these problems?

Relationship Management and Contractor Motivation

Introduction

It is often said that, when entering into contracts, contracts officers should be aware of the type of relationship that they aim to develop with the contractor. They should then try to ensure that, whatever type of relationship is developed, it is maintained throughout the contract's running time. The relationship 'concept' is a way of describing the nature of dealings that contracts officer and contractor have between them and there is quite a wide range of possible relationships. These range from 'adversarial' at one end of the spectrum to 'co-destiny' at the other, as we will see later.

Whatever kind of relationship a contracts officer enters into with a contractor, there is usually need to motivate the contractor so that they bring the contract to a successful conclusion. This means that, ideally, all of the contract goals will have been achieved. There is a perception that mere payment should be enough to motivate contractors. However, other means of motivation might be considered useful when the contracts officer wants contributions from the contractor such as:

- Suggestions relating to how contractual objectives might be achieved.

- Innovations which might assist better contract completion than was otherwise expected.

We will consider ways of motivating contractors later in this chapter.

The Range of Relationships

As stated above, there is a range of possible relationships that a contracts officer might have with a contractor and this range can be illustrated by the following diagram:

$$\longleftarrow \qquad \longrightarrow$$

Distant relationships		**Closer relationships**

Adversarial	Transactional	Single Sourced Strategic Alliance
		Co-destiny
Arm's length	Closer tactical Outsourcing	Partnership

Before we go any further it is worth considering what each of these terms mean:

- **Adversarial** – a relationship of almost open hostility, characterised by a total lack of trust between the parties. This type of relationship is usually accompanied by a very tight contract that prescribes almost every aspect of the dealings between the parties. Such relationships often come into being when the contracts officer has few, if any, alternative contractors and/or when the contractor does not trust the contracts officer for reasons such as poor payment or frequent changes of specification. It is, generally, not the type of relationship to aim for but a contracts officer might find themselves in a situation where there is no real alternative.

- **'Arm's length' relationship**. This is the 'traditional' relationship between contracts officer and seller. Price is the dominant variable and there is no attempt to build up trust or long-term commitment.

- **Transactional relationship.** This is similar to 'arm's length' and is based on the idea of purchasing as an exchange of goods or services in return for payment. The 'Dictionary of Purchasing and Supply' by Compton & Jessop defines this relationship as **"a relationship between contracts officer and seller whereby 2 parties do not get closely involved with each other but simply exchange goods or services for payment"**. It focuses on the successful completion of ordinary transactions for low-value, low-risk goods and services purchased from a competent contractor. With low value purchases, or purchases of relatively low importance to the buying organisation, it is not worth committing time and effort to closer relationships. Alternatively, when the product or service is available from a large number of competing contractors, it is possible that contractors will be unable to differentiate their product or service on grounds other than on the bases of price and availability. In this situation, the potential for securing joint benefits through investing in a collaborative relationship is likely to be limited and a transactional relationship might be appropriate. Another scenario for the adoption of transactional relationships might be where the purchasing organisation believes that a collaborative, win/win relationship would be appropriate but where the contractor is wedded to a traditional, transactional-type relationship. Examples of purchasing situations suitable for transactional relationships might be as in this list:
  - Building services.
  - Commodity goods.
  - The supply of goods available from a wide range of sources.
  - Some types of transport service such as parcel delivery and occasional road haulage.

Another situation suitable for transactional relationships might be in industries that are concerned with rapidly evolving technology. In such situations, whilst purchasers might need to work closely with contractors on the development of important and valuable components or sub-assemblies, there is also a transactional element to the relationship because it will be limited to the useful life of the contractor's technology. When technology moves on, it might be necessary to use a new contractor and each new technology step is likely to involve the 'shakeout' of certain old contractors and the addition of new ones.

- **Closer tactical.** It can be very difficult to differentiate between some of the stages in this 'spectrum' but this is similar to the transactional relationship but might involve a greater level of requesting and being granted, 'favours' from the contractor such as assistance with technical questions.

- **Single sourced.** This is a situation where a contractor has shown over time that they are reliable in terms of quality and service and, at the same time, are competitive in terms of price with other contractors. In such situations, the contracts officer might choose to purchase 100% of their requirement of the item/service from that contractor. This, by definition, means that any relationship developed is going to be reasonably collaborative. Alternatively, such a relationship might develop because the contractor is the only practical supply option and this is likely to mean that a reasonably close relationship would need to be developed although there is a fairly obvious element of 'force' in this.

- **Outsourcing.** Outsourcing is increasingly popular today and if important services are outsourced, it should go without saying that a close relationship needs to be developed with the service provider to ensure that the service is performed properly and to the required standard on a daily basis and that any required changes to the service content and/or schedule can be dealt with smoothly.

- **Strategic alliance.** This is a term employed where contracts officer and seller organisations co-operate closely on the development, manufacture or supply of a product or service. This suggests a 'cross-functional' relationship where (e.g.) engineers in both organisations collaborate with each other rather than a situation where only the contracts officer and sales contact work together. The purpose here is to enable both organisations to move forward together in way that is, to a great extent, mutually dependent. Both parties might mutually develop joint initiatives such as cost cutting or quality improvement.

- **Partnership sourcing.** This is an approach to sourcing through which mutually profitable long-term relationships between contractors and their customers are sought, based on openness and trust. It is important to note that this approach is not intended to allow 'partners' to become relaxed and perhaps therefore less competitive, but instead to become more competitive through co-operation in the avoidance of waste, problem solving, etc. Partnership sourcing has been defined as: A commitment by customers/contractors, regardless of size, to a long-term relationship based on clear mutually agreed objectives to strive for world class capability and performance. Characteristics of partnership are identified as follows:
  - Top level commitment.
  - Openness and trust.
  - Clear joint objectives between contracts officer and contractor.

- Long-term relationship.
- Pro active not reactive.
- Total quality management.
- Working together.
- Flexibility.
- Involvement of all disciplines.

The advantages for purchasers are:
- Faster product and service development.
- Improved quality.
- Delivery on time.
- Designing cost out.

For contractors, the advantages are:
- Long-term-agreement.
- Improved management capability.
- Marketing advantage.
- Improved technological capability.
- Financial stability, including payment on time.

The advantages for both parties are:
- Reduced total cost, profitable for both parties.
- Lower inventories and reduced logistics.

- **Co-destiny.** This where two companies' future is very closely, if not inextricably, linked. An example commonly given is that of British Airways and Boeing where each party would find survival difficult (although not necessarily impossible) without the other.

Relationship Management

This should be considered no matter what kind of relationship has been entered into although it comes to the fore much more in 'closer' relationships. It should mean that management attention is focused on the relationship and interactions between a company and its contractors. It often means that greater responsibility is passed to a contractor in terms of successful completion of the contract.

Why is there so much interest in relationships?

Traditionally, relationships between contracts officer and contractor tended to be adversarial or 'arm's length' in nature. In other words, there was no kind of 'getting together', no concept of joint problem solving or a joint focus on cost cutting or any of the joint approaches that characterise much of today's business world.

Essentially, the contractor supplied the goods, hopefully on time and of the right quality, charged the agreed price and the contracts officer paid the contractor and that was the sum total of dealings between the two parties. If the contractor failed in some way the contracts officer simply found another contractor and tendering was regularly used to try to identify a cheaper contractor than the current one and if such a contractor thee found, business would be moved to them from the existing contractor as soon as possible.

So why is there so much interest in partnerships today? The answer to this question is, to some extent, situational in that different contracts officers and sellers have different reasons for thinking about relationships and considering closer relationships. Typical reasons for this greater interest in relationships include but are not limited to:

- A greater dependency on contractors that own technology, which may be exemplified by patents, copyright, registered designs or other forms of intellectual property.

- The growth of buying-in of important items rather than making them in house.

- The growth and development of outsourcing.

- The increasing need and desire to purchase services, particularly specialist services.

- The belief that working more closely with contractors can lead to joint initiatives on such issues as cost cutting and general problem solving, a good example here being the growth, in the manufacturing sector of the use of Early Contractor Involvement (or ESI) at the design stage of new products.

- The fact that, in some markets, there is a concentration of a smaller number of powerful contractors. In this situation, contracts officers needs to work with the contractor rather than against them.

- The increasing interest in lean supply. The need to try to drive down costs and remove everything that doesn't add value from the supply chain suggests that contracts officers need to work more closely with contractors at every level in the supply chain.

- The supply chain philosophy, which falls short of lean supply, still needs a degree of collaboration at all levels in the supply chain.

All of this suggests that the only type of relationship worth discussing is the collaborative, partnership type. This is not true, however. A collaborative relationship might be appropriate in the situations we have just mentioned but there are many other types of relationship, generally characterised as being more adversarial, that may be perfectly valid in different situations.

The Waitrose supermarket procurement team has secured supplier investment to develop new refrigeration technology that avoids using a lot of harmful chemicals. A water-and-propane-based system is being introduced to in-store refrigeration to help reduce the company's environmental impact.

How relationships are formed (targeting)

Relationships do not just 'happen' accidentally. Whilst it may be true that relationships may develop in a naturalistic way, the idea of them just 'happening' is not true. Contracts officers should ask themselves: "What kind of relationship should I be aiming for in this particular contract situation?" This introduces the idea of relationship targeting.

Many people view the concept of partnership relationships as being a good one but there is still room for the adversarial relationship. There is evidence of some contracts officers entering into partnership agreements with contractors and withdrawing from them because they thee not working. So, how do we decide which basic approach to take in order to develop a relationship that is relevant to the particular contract?

An approach that many people use is known as Procurement Targeting. This suggests that the contracts officer should analyse all items purchased against two variables: Supply Risk and Level of Spend, sometimes know as 'Impact on Profitability'. We should note that it is the items/services that we purchase that are so divided, not, at this stage, the contractors. Supply risk usually derives from the number of contractors in the market, so that a market with few contractors would be a 'high risk' one, although risk can also derive from issues such as the contracts officer's reputation. Reputation will derive from such issues as whether the contracts officer is a 'prestige' customer and whether they settle invoices on time (see 'Contractor Preference' below).

The two variables of risk and spend can be plotted on a matrix, often known as the Kraljic matrix after the writer who devised it.

High

Bottleneck   Critical

Supply
Market
Risk

Routine   Leverage

Low

Low   High

Routine items. Typically, these will be MRO items and consumables, although they are not limited to these items and will have low value and annual spend and many contractors. In this situation, we do not need to adopt a partnership approach, nor is it worth spending much time changing from one contractor to another and carrying out competitive bidding exercises, etc. Thus, the general rule here is to find a reliable contractor for each category of item in this box, for example stationery, negotiate a contract and automate the purchasing process as much as possible, using blanket orders, direct requisitioning, consignment stocking and so on.

Leverage items. Typically, these are items where there are many contractors and we have a high annual spend. Examples might be standard components used in large quantity. The nature of such markets means that we have a high degree of power and we can use this power to maximise the contribution that supplies management can make to profitability, hence the name 'leverage' items because here we can maximise the profit leverage effect. When buying this category of item, there is nothing to stop we from moving from contractor to contractor if the existing one does not give we the service we want, using competitive bidding to compare one contractor against another and changing them, as necessary. In other words, an adversarial approach may well pay dividends here.

Bottleneck items. This is the reverse situation of leverage items. Typically, there will be few contractors and we will not be spending much money on the item. Thus, contractors will have little motivation to go out of their way to be 'good' contractors. The usual view is that, for this type of purchase, we try to find a good contractor whom we can, at least, make understand the requirements and agree a contract for a reasonably long period of time, perhaps 2 to 3 years, to give a reasonable overall value to keep the contractor interested to some extent.

Critical items (sometimes known as 'strategic'). These are items where there are few contractors but on which we are spending a great deal of money. This means that we need the contractor we choose and they need we. It is in this quadrant of the matrix where we try to develop partnerships with chosen contractors after we have taken steps to find one that we can work with and trust.

Some writers have doubts about the Kraljic approach to procurement targeting and suggest that there might be other methods of doing this. One suggestion is that we should look at what we want from the purchasing operation. For example, if the company is trying to work towards TQM or lean supply, we need to adopt an approach to contractors and therefore, a relationship that will contribute to such objectives. Other factors might include:

- **The geographical location** – it is always more difficult to enter into close relationships with a contractor that is geographically distant than with those who are closer at hand.

- The **attitudes and perceptions of contractors** – e.g. some contractors might be more or less willing than others to enter into close relationships.

- **Final customer perceptions** – some end customers might feel that close relationships in the supply chain might not be in their best interests.

- **Symbolic factors** such as whether the two companies want to investigate the possibility of (e.g.) sharing advertising/ publicity.

- **Government regulations** that, in some cases, might limit the possibility of the development of close relationships, such as in the public sector.

- **Supply market conditions** – e.g. in highly competitive markets, with many contractors, contracts officers might be less inclined to enter into a close relationship with a single contractor.

- **The existence of trust** – this is a prerequisite for the development of close relationships.

- The **ability to transact online** – this might "drive" a closer relationship because the ability to transact online gives we the ability effectively to "automate" dealings with the contractor. A close relationship would be necessary for this situation to operate satisfactorily.

All of this supposes that the contracts officer can drive the kind of relationship developed with a contractor but what might the contractor think about it? We can't develop any kind of collaborative relationship with an unwilling contractor and it may not necessarily regard the business as worth a collaborative relationship. This idea introduces the Contractor Preference Model. This illustrates how a contractor might view we as a purchaser based on two variables: the value of the account; in other words, how much money we spend with them and: the 'attractiveness' as a customer. Attractiveness covers such issues as whether we are a 'prestige' customer or whether we cause the contractor problems by, for example, not being a good payer, making frequent changes to quantities and specifications, cancelling orders and so on.

Contractor Preference Model

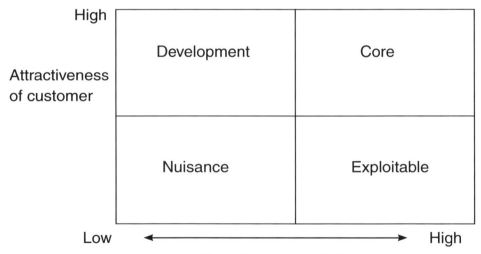

As the diagram shows: if our account is of low value and we are considered to be an unattractive customer, we will be considered a nuisance and it is unlikely that a contractor would want to enter into a collaborative relationship because, frankly, they will not be bothered whether we buy from them or not. Similarly, if the organisation is considered 'exploitable' – the contractor would look to adopt an adversarial relationship with the organisation. On the other hand, if the contractor considered the business to be 'core' or worthy of development, it is likely that they would want to develop a close relationship.

The nature of a relationship might change over time. This might happen 'naturally' because, for example, our requirement of what a contractor provides decreases so that a previously collaborative relationship might become more distant and vice versa. Alternatively, we might want to change it because we are not happy with the way it is working. Alternatively, we might realise over time that a contractor with which we have a transactional relationship is very good and could make a greater contribution to our organisation and we might want to develop a more collaborative relationship.

This introduces the concept of managing risk in commercial relationships. This usually comes into play when a collaborative relationship has been entered into and we want to monitor how it is progressing. This might involve a fairly traditional risk management process, Potential risks such as quality or service deterioration need to be identified, how likely they are to occur and what likely impact they might have should be identified. An example here might be quality: if a contractor's quality deteriorates, it might have a serious effect on the quality of our product and impair the standing in the supply market. Questions that should be asked are:

- 'How likely is this to happen?

- Why might it happen?

- How serious in terms of our supply market would it be?

- What can we do about it if it does happen?

If the answer to these questions is that the problem is highly likely to happen, that it will have disastrous consequences and would be difficult to correct, we must have ways available of reducing the risk. This would often involve having a back-up contractor and might lead we have a reasonably distant relationship with the original contractor so that another one could be called upon if necessary. Alternatively, of course, such risk identification might lead we to try to develop a closer relationship with the contractor with a view to mutual problem solving.

The behaviour of both parties is important here. A collaborative relationship of any kind cannot exist with only one party being willing to collaborate with the other. Such behaviours concern issues such as the contractor's costs and contracts officer's profit (contractors want to be sure that the contracts officer is not making excessive profits out of their diligence at cost reduction and reduction of waste). In today's world, another issue here might be environmental friendliness.

Many writers on this subject take the view that we must 'manage' relationships so that any one relationship continues over time to provide the benefits that we are looking for. 'Managing' involves understanding the contractor's requirements and wishes from the relationship and doing the best to accommodate them, as well as holding frequent meetings with them to deal with any issues or problems that might arise and reach mutually acceptable conclusions.

Motivation of Contractors

In the introduction to this chapter it was stated that, if a contracts officer wishes a contractor to contribute such things as innovation or suggestions for improvement, it would often be necessary to motivate the contractor. It might appear that payment for goods and/ or services provided should be sufficient motivation but research and experience shows that motivation can be improved in other ways. Motivation can be linked to relationships and relationship development.

Maslow's 'Hierarchy of Needs'

This is a famous piece of research that is usually related to personal motivation of employees. However, its principles can be applied to contractors and their motivation. Maslow postulated that most human needs can be classified into one of five categories and that individuals thee first driven to satisfy their most basic needs (e.g., food would take precedence over safety and security if one thee hungry and felt unsafe). However, once a lothe level need was satisfied, individuals would be driven toward the next higher level need. The 'hierarchy' is as follows with links to motivation of contractors:

- Physiological Needs (e.g., food, water, air, shelter): for contractors this would be represented by timely payment of invoices which would go a long way towards keeping the contractor in business.

- Safety and Security (protection, stability): for contractors, this might be the promise of future business which should provide a degree of stability.

- Social (affection, friendship and belonging): for contractors, this one is a little more difficult but would include the development of a closer relationship which should lead to the contractor being considered as a 'trusted' contractor. This should give the contractor confidence that it would continue to gain business from the contracts officer over time.

- Ego (prestige, success, self-respect): this might include the contractor's becoming a 'partner' (i.e. having a 'partnership' type relationship with the contracts officer). This should mean that both contracts officer and contractor would be able to work together over time and that the contractor would be able to use the relationship for positive publicity. If this thee the case, it should mean that the contractor's business would continue to thrive.

- Self-actualisation (self-fulfilment): this might include the contractor's ability to advertise itself as a key contractor to the contracts officer's organisation which, particularly if the contracts officer is a 'prestige' customer, would give the contractor considerable publicity and greatly enhance its reputation. Again, this would give the contractor great confidence in gaining much business from its general market and not only make it successful but allow it to grow.

Methods of Motivating Contractors

Research shows that the contract structure and incentives can have a major impact on contractors' motivation to innovate. Joint funding of investments and the award of longer-term contracts are powerful incentives. This can particularly be the case in hard economic times because such joint funding and contract award can give a contractor a degree of certainty about the future of its business.

Other means of motivating contractors, in the case of high performing ones, would be:

- Make public recognition of the contractor's service, abilities, etc. This would allow the contractor to use such an award as part of its advertising and publicity.

- Give something like a '5 star award' to the contractor, again for high level services rendered. This could also be used for publicity by the contractor.

Chapter Summary

In this chapter we have considered the nature of relationships; relationship management and motivation of contractors.

- There is a wide range of relationships from adversarial at one end of the spectrum to 'co-destiny' at the other. Contracts officers must try to choose which relationship would be best with each contractor, a process which can be quite complex involving targeting.

- Once a relationship has been established, it is important to 'manage' it to ensure that it functions in a way that encourages the contractor to continue to supply in the manner required. This is particularly true of relationships at the closer end of the spectrum.

- Another way of ensuring that contractors continue to supply in the manner required is to motivate them on an ongoing basis. Again, this is particularly true where relationships are closer.

Case Study

SAS Oil and Gas is a large international energy company based in the UK. The company employs many contractors to undertake a wide range of works and to provide many different services including IT, maintenance, transport and many others. SAS strategy with contracts is to award to the lowest priced technically acceptable bidder and it maintains a large list of approved contractors.

Currently SAS has a problem with some of its smaller construction contractors, in particular Patel Construction Services. On site the contractor is reluctant to be cooperative

---

or flexible and rarely goes beyond meeting its very basic contractor obligations. This leads to delays, cost over runs and poor quality work on occasions. This makes life difficult for the end users.

All contractors are closely supervised by SAS contract officers and at the weekly review meeting (which sometimes the contractor does not attend) often degenerates into a "blame" allocation session, whereby the contract officer berates the contractor. The contractor's staffs are not well regarded by SAS contract management and any form of recognition or "praise" is avoided, as management believe this would only encourage the contractor to seek higher rates.

The contractor is well paid by local standards and the settlement of accounts is usually quite prompt, although occasional disputes or a lack of minor work order documentation from the contracts officer can hold up payment of Patel's invoices. The contractor has a contract that is due for review in 12 months; SAS only allow contracts to be let for a maximum of 24 months. The SAS contracting cycle can take up to 11 months and the contracts team have already started the process of re letting this contract.

On site, it is the policy of SAS to keep contractors and their own staff quite separate. They feel that being too close might breed contempt. Contractors have to wear bright yellow jackets, while staff wears a more attractive blue. Catering for all contractors is provided by Low Cost Catering – LCC ltd, in a large huts, while staff meals are provided by La Cucina, a well known French catering company. The company places a lot of emphasis on safety, especially as contractor accidents tends to hold up operations and cost SAS money.

There have been occasions when Patel have made suggestions on how to undertake work in a more cost effective manner, but these have not been taken up by SAS. The Head of SAS Contracts states "The contractor's role is to do the work as directed, any ideas they have will no doubt cost us money!"

Task
How would you change things at SAS?

Measuring Contract Performance

Definitions

The measurement of contract performance provides a way to determine what has been accomplished and can serve as a basis for deciding when those accomplishments deserve special recognition, in the form of incentive payments, awards and contractor recognition systems. Within the context of contract the performance measurement process, measuring means determining the level of performance by judging the quality, quantity, timeliness, and/or cost effectiveness of against a set of pre determined standards and outcomes.

The key aims of an effective system of monitoring contract performance are:

- Ensuring delivering the outputs to the required standard.
- Ensuring contractors are meeting their contractual obligations.
- Early identification of problems to ensure prompt remedial action.
- Price and payment terms are adhered to.
- Verification of performance linked incentive payments.

This enables the contract and the contractors to be carefully controlled and monitored.

Levels of Performance Management

The effective performance of any contracting organization depends on the contribution of a range of activities. There are three or four levels of performance management in the OGC model framework below, some organizations may combine the strategic level with the organization's priorities level.

Organisation's priorities: at the highest level performance management is rooted in the organisation's long term business strategy. Measures at this level are of impact, resource utilisation and service improvement.

Strategic level performance management: at this level the management concern is from an "outside in" as well as an internal perspective. Measures are of outcome, such as volume and value of service take-up, upward trends for inclusion, staff and users' satisfaction.

Programme level performance management: performance management at this level is focused on the desired results of programmes of change, to demonstrate what has been accomplished. The measures used would include those stated in individual business cases. Benefits management would help to determine if these are achieved.

Tactical or operational service level performance management: here the management focus is concerned with service delivery and outputs, using conventional service level agreement approaches and related measures of aspects such as volumes and quality.

Contracting Key Performance Indicators (KPIs) may feature at all levels of the framework and are not limited to the tactical or operational elements, for example developing innovative solutions with contractors to gain a competitive advantage could be deemed to be a strategic goal.

Monitoring Performance

Monitoring Performance against key indicators is becoming a standard feature in many contracts. The contractor's performance must be assessed objectively against clearly agreed standards and targets set out in the contract.

Contract officers are responsible for developing an effective system of performance measurement.

A recent report by the UK National Audit Office states that the UK Ministry of Defence is facing "considerable challenges" in its supply chain and is failing to hit its own performance targets – making deliveries on time in only 54% cases. The highest priority items sent by air are expected to arrive in military theatre within five days but this was only achieved in around a third of cases. The report also found a large variation in the time it takes similar items to move through the supply chain.

Key Performance Indicators (KPIs)

Key Performance Indicators are used by contracting organizations to measure and evaluate the success of a particular activity within the contract. This can include the repeated achievement of some level of contractual obligation or outcomes. Therefore choosing the right KPIs is reliant upon having a good understanding of what is important to the organization and what has been contracted for.

Performance Review Meetings

The contract officer should undertake periodic formal review meetings of their contractors performance. These meetings should involve senior personnel from both the client and the contractor. The aim of the formal review process is to:

- Provide an overview of the operation of the whole contract
- Allow any outstanding issues or problems to be managed in an informed and effective manner
- Anticipate potential problems
- Minimise their incidence and severity

Contract Management Dashboards

In terms of management information systems, a dashboard can be contract management interface that is designed to be easy to read and understand. In the case of contractual KPI this might include trends in delivery or cost management measures. The key advantage is that access to information is immediate and transparent. This allows for effect management and tracking of the contract and the contractors performance.

The benefits of Contract Management Dashboards can include:

- Visual presentation of performance measures.
- Ability to identify and correct negative trends.
- Measure efficiencies/inefficiencies.
- Ability to generate detailed reports showing new trends.
- Ability to make more informed decisions based on collected business intelligence.
- Align strategies and organizational goals.
- Saves time compared to running multiple reports.
- Gain total visibility of all systems instantly.
- Quick identification of data outliers and correlations.

What to Measure?

The OGC Contract Management Guidelines advise that measuring service quality means creating and using quality metrics. These measurements allow the quality of a service to be measured and therefore potentially improved. The aspects of service quality that can be assessed include:

- completeness
- availability
- capacity
- reliability
- flexibility
- timeliness
- responsiveness
- security
- standards
- usability

- accuracy
- audit ability

A very common method for choosing KPIs is to apply a management framework such as the Balanced scorecard.

The Balance Score Card Institute in the USA defines BSC as a strategic planning and management system that is used extensively in business and industry, government, and non profit organizations worldwide to align business activities to the vision and strategy of the organization, improve internal and external communications, and monitor organization performance against strategic goals. It was originated by Drs. Robert Kaplan (Harvard Business School) and David Norton as a performance measurement framework that added strategic non-financial performance measures to traditional financial metrics to give managers and executives a more 'balanced' view of organizational performance. This logic can be adapted the specifics of measuring the performance of a contract, in that we may need to measure a wide range of metrics, rather than the traditional time, quality ad cost performance elements. This could include innovation, relationships, CSR and many others.

A working example of a KPI measurement system is the DPSS KPI model©.

This is based upon the idea that the organisation needs to identify and measure a wide range of metrics, but also that they need to have a means by which some of the more subjective elements can be measured consistently. This especially is critical when a number of stakeholders are involved in the assessment process.

The DPSS model makes use of the "Key Statement" method, whereby the standard of performance required and achieved are clearly defined, for example the metric to measure contractor innovation would be presented as:

1. Resistant to change. No new ideas or suggestions put forward. No evidence of desire to innovate.

2. Willing to change but no viable ideas put forward, lack of focus.

3. Some ideas put forward occasionally, on an ad hoc basis.

4. Constantly looking for new ways of doing things, people and processes and putting viable suggestions forward.

5. Highly innovative and pro active approach, new ideas that can be implemented, highly motivated approach to drive through new arrangements, part of a planned internal process.

The simple 1-5 scoring system allows all the stakeholders to assess and score the contractors performance, against a pre agreed level, in the context of the nature of the contract. Therefore in a simple routine contract to clean the office windows, the contracts officer would not burden the contractor (and thus increase costs) by setting the required level of service for innovation at 5 – for the simple reason that as a routine and well established task the opportunities for a "Highly innovative approach" could be said to be limited.

Once the desired and required level of service per metric is establish and the process of assessment takes place, the contracts officer has a clean comparison between the desirable and essential levels of service and the actual performance achieved and thus appropriate actions can be taken. The model includes many elements of service provision including:

Flexibility
1. Very rigid approach, unwilling to react to changing situation, seeks to only to meet contract obligations.

2. Limited flexibility only when forced to deal with changing situation, unwilling approach.

3. Flexible on most occasions, seeks to interpret the contract to the benefit of both parties.

4. Very flexible and co operative in the vast majority of situations, contractor seeks to be willing partner and strives to delight the client.

5. Very flexible, always willing to respond to changing requirements.

Relationships

1. Poor, constant conflict, complete ongoing lack of communication, adversarial, non-cooperation.

2. Limited contact, adversarial, some conflict, focuses on obligations.

3. Common understanding of requirement and needs, recognition of need to co-operate, willing to negotiate conflicts/disputes, exchange of value constructively, trust.

4. Mature, professional/commercial approach, recognition of contribution of both sides to manage the relationships, nurturing and developing the relationship, free flow of information/ideas, concerning, free to open discussions, candid feedback, able to cope with stresses and strains.

5. Harmonious symbolic relationship, confident, jointly agrees objectives, mutual risk and rewards approach, commitment, constantly seeking opportunities to eliminate NVAs and to add value.

Health, Safety and the Environment

1. Non-compliance which could lead to serious injury, major environmental excursion or improvement/enforcement notice.

2. Non-compliance which could lead to injury or damage to plant,

minor environmental excursion or lead to regulator raising issues.

3. Compliance with legislation and station/contractor procedures.

4. Proactive approach leading to standards above legislative or station/contractor requirements. Developing positive safety culture.

5. Innovative approach. Excellent standards. Institutionalised safety culture.

Responsiveness

1. Failure to respond to any requests for information, support or any assistance, constant reference to contract terms.

2. Reluctant to respond, constant reference to the contractual obligations, unwilling to freely respond, very passive approach.

3. Adequate response, more flexible approach, positive attitude, commercial interpretation of contract obligations.

4. High levels of responsiveness, being proactive, positive approach, appreciate the added value of being responsive.

5. Exceeding requirements, very proactive, seeks to respond before requested, culture of customer delight.

Flexibility

1. Very rigid approach, unwilling to react to changing situation, seeks to only to meet contract obligations.

2. Limited flexibility only when forced to deal with changing situation, unwilling approach.

3. Flexible on most occasions, seeks to interpret the contract to the benefit of both parties.

4. Very flexible and co operative in the vast majority of situations, contractor seeks to be willing partner and strives to delight the client.

5. Very flexible, always willing to respond to changing requirements.

Site Concentric

1. Complete lack of appreciation of key issue, no pre-planning for local requirements, hide behind contract, no recognition of issue. lack of sensitivity. Recognised issues, wouldn't/couldn't resolve, adopts adversarial. seeks constant support from Supply Chain team.

2. Recognition of issues, some effort to resolve, appropriate actions taken, ad hoc response, reactive.

3. Proactive approach, committed to dealing with the issue, planned response, appreciative of issues, professional approach.

4. Multi-site process, total understanding, conflict/resolution, diplomacy, appropriate skills sets, sensitivity, very proactive, consistent, pre visit research.

5. Excellent site relationship management.

Performance

1. Work not started, complete programme failure, not to QA well below standard/cost overruns, excessive demands for variations.

2. Work not delivered to programme, but cost management achieved, still quality issues to address.

3. Work to QA but not to programme but steps taken to bring it back.

4. Work completed to programme at cost and quality.

5. Work provided delights the customer.

Quality

1. Quality of work far below standard or delivered not at required standard, not fit for purpose.

2. Quality of work less than satisfactory needs re working and improvement, lack of trust/confidence in contractors outputs.

3. Quality of work is adequate, but still significant opportunities for improvement.

4. Quality of work meets client expectations, some confidence in the contractors output, significant progress toward fit for purpose.

5. Quality is deemed to be totally fit for purpose.

Cost Management

1. Complete lack of cost control, cost overruns, variations, imposed cost increases, failure to meet budget targets.

2. Lack of transparency, failure to justify cost increases, seeking variations to cost.

3. Good cost control, budget targets met on significant occasions.

4. Effective cost management, professional approach, commercial treatment of cost variations.

5. Total cost control, transparency, co operation in the management of costs.

Program or Project Completion
1. Non-completion or delivery of task.

2. Failure to deliver on time, significant overrun, lack of prior warning, major commercial impact, critical material or service, major input required by contract management team.

3. Delivery late, but not significant to cause a major commercial impact and additional input and resource required by contract management team.

4. Delivery on time and to programme.

5. Delivery offered in advance, if required, minimal input from contract management team, seamless process from contract award to delivery of service.

Flow of Information
1. Inconsistent, ambiguous, inappropriate, noise, non-factual, non-productive, misleading, unknown/non-existent, no system.

2. Known information, unstructured, unfocused, non-conformance, to standard, ad hoc, acknowledge need for system.

3. Formal process to standard, structured, ad hoc, untimely.

4. Timely, standard, targeted, formal, known audience, committed.

5. Clear, concise, accurate, well communicated, timely, standard format, channel, audience, 360° (close loop) communication, acknowledgement, factual, follow up.

The Challenge of Developing Effective KPI Systems

The challenges facing contract officers in relation to KPI is often that of too many individual metrics and the late reporting of results. KPIs are meant to be regular and provide up to date feed back, which will enable the contract officer to take corrective action, if necessary. Having a multitude of metrics tends to inhibit their effective use, mainly due to information overload combined with a complex and time consuming process of collection leads to delays in reporting.

Stages in Developing KPIs

The process of developing appropriate contractual KPI can include the following:

- **Identify critical success factors** – what will really determine the successful performance of the contract? for example in a maintenance services contract reliable call out times could be the critical factor for the key stakeholder, therefore the measurement and tracking of this metric is a priority.

- **Determine measures of success or improvements for each factor/area** – this could include time, customer feed back, cost management, flexibility and innovation.

- **Develop KPIs with key stakeholders** – it is critical that all KPI are development in co operation with the key stakeholders, to ensure that what is vital to the internal customer and others, is reflected in the measurement system.

- **Agree actual KPIs with key stakeholders** – for example is a oil rig drilling contract, actual metres drilled per hour could be a critical KPI.

- **Monitor, review and control**

A major UK local council states "The contractor must be capable of delivering the requirements of the contract. You should be aware that contract conditions will be strictly applied especially with regard to quality and general performance. The council is continuously striving to improve its own performance and it expects its contractors to do the same. By the same token, the council will look seriously at the position of any contractor that fails to perform to the levels required."

To support this rigorous approach a system of clear contractual KPIs needed to be developed.

Why Do Contractors Fail to Perform?

There are many reasons why the contractor may fail to achieve their targets as expressed in the KPI – some can systemic others and due to external factors but mainly the reasons have their roots in the original contracting process and a failure to follow the dpss Six-S model. (see chapter 2). The factors that can result in contractors (and contracts) not performing to target can also include:

- Unrealistic targets – in terns of expectations of the client in terms of what can be delivered and expectations of the contractors as to what they can deliver.

- Lack of adequate contractor resources – the contractor has not truly understood the requirement and has therefore failed to deploy sufficient resources to meet the expectations of the client.

- The contractors adopts a strategy of lowest price offer to secure the business and then is unable to deliver to the required standard and thus fails to achieve the KPI.

Chapter Summary

In this chapter we have looked at the meaning of performance measurement and concept of KPI. We have reviewed the methods and models regarding the measurement of contractor's performance.

The chapter examines what needs to be measured in terms of contracts and contractors and that these measures can relate to strategic and operational aspects of the organisations aims and objectives.

The chapter also looks at the process of developing effective KPI and the related challenges.

Case Study

Alpha is a large oil and gas company, based in the UAE. Many of its operations are off shore. The company has to cater for a large workface made up of both staff and contractors. The provision of high quality meals and service is a key priority for Alpha and it is seen as part of the employee's compensation package. The catering has been outsourced to Meals International, a local company based in Dubia. The contract stipulates that the company has to provide breakfast, lunch and dinner to all employees, plus occasional additional services like catering for meetings, parties and company social events. Meals International have a good reputation and they won the contract as the lowest priced technically acceptable bidder.

Ali is the contract administrator for the catering contract and he has some concerns. Alpha came to the contract with a wide range of KPI(s) imbedded; this impressed Ali at the technical evaluation stage. The results from recent employee feed back surveys, whilst they do not actually complain; they only rate the experience as "just satisfactory" Ali is concerned by this given the amount of time and effort that goes into collecting and monitoring the KPI(s) which are need to calculate the contractors generous bonus. He recently reviewed the contractors KPI(s) which included:

- Quality of the plates and cutlery
- Space between the tables
- Canteen décor
- Neatness of staff uniforms
- Prompt submission of invoices
- Stockroom housekeeping
- Health and Safety – reported loss time incidents

All these are achieved by the contractor, almost every week. On the rare occasions when the contractor fails to meet his targets a long and heated debate normally ensues. One of the key KPI is that of HSE. Ali is please that there have been no reported incidents or near misses for the past 12 months, although he cannot help noticing that staff display many cuts and bruises, apparently accidents that occurred at home. One contractor employee recently broke his leg while on site, but states that he did it playing football during his break.

Task
Task Critically evaluate the current KPI system.

9 Variations and Claims

Introduction

According to the Centre for Education in the Built Environment at Cardiff University, "In a perfect world changes will be confined to the planning stages". This is any Contract Manager's goal, but we have to accept and examine:

- Why changes to contracts happen.
- The resulting effect on the contract through variations or claims.
- The measures needed in order to avoid the worst consequences of change.

The Difference between Variations and Claims

We all recognise that however much careful effort is put into ensuring that the specification or SOW is fully, clearly, concisely and unambiguously defined, there will almost be certainly be changes required either to the scope or the method of working. Change happens, for reasons which may be good, unforeseeable or just plain lack of forethought or incompetence. However, before we examine such changes in detail, we need to be very clear about the different ways in which change may come about.

A Contract Variation or **"Variation"** is a change to the overall scope of the contract and occurs when the customer (or an individual nominated on its behalf, such as the Contract Manager) issues a request to the contractor to vary a contract that has already been awarded. This could consist of an instruction to increase (or decrease) the quantity such as changing the scope of construction of 100 houses to 110 or to add (or remove) a specific element of the contract such as the addition of storage compound to a requirement for a warehouse. The key feature here is that the customer is getting more or less of something, for which there will probably be a requirement for a change in the contract price. Variations are sometimes called "Contract Amendments", but care must be taken to differentiate this form an amendment to the conditions of contract (such as changing a guarantee period from 36 to 24 months). In this case the change does not affect the scope of work and can only be made through agreement by both parties. A variation can be issued by the customer if the contract allows for such a provision in the form of a variation clause.

A Contractual Claim or **"Claim"** however results normally, when the contractor is asked by the customer or forced to by causes within in the customer's control or third parties outside the contractor's control to carry out the contract in a manner, which will lead to him additional cost, through circumstances that he could not have reasonably anticipated. For example, if the contract had specified that the contractor could only carry out the work between 9.00 a.m. and 5.00 p.m Monday to Friday and is then asked to complete the contract using evening and weekend working. He may be entitled to receive additional payments, if the contract allows such claims to be submitted and he can prove that additional costs have been incurred. In this particular instance, the customer is not getting any additional benefit as would be the case with a variation. He is merely compensating the contractor for additional costs incurred.

The situation can become confused, when a request for additional work causes disruption to the contractor, which may mean that any additional payment may be part variation and part claim.

It is also worth briefly noting that another type of claim known as "ex-gratia" where the contractor is one not entitled to receive any form of payment in accordance with the contract, but there may still good reason to make such a payment for reasons such as:

- Undue hardship will be suffered by the contractor, which may prejudice his ability to complete successfully.

- The customer having some sympathy with the contractor, believing the contract may not have dealt him a fair hand.

- Showing a willingness not to stick rigidly to the contract may lead to a concession in the future by the contractor.

- The facts of any claim may be so costly or time-consuming to ascertain, that it is more practical just to agree a reasonable sum.

Variations

Causes

Having established what a variation is, we should look at the causes of which there are many:

- The original specification may be inadequate. This may because an element of it is unclear or ambiguous, so the contractor can reasonably argue that a variation is required to fill this gap.

- Customers can sometime change their mind or wish to add additional scope. This may be through genuine need, but also may be as a result of a "nice to have" culture or subtle persuasion from a contractor of the value of extra features.

- A culture within the customer of continuous change.

- Leaving important details 'to be sorted out later'.

- There may be a new innovation that can be taken advantage of.

- The customer may need to delete items due to lack of funding.

- There may be external factors, which necessarily change the requirements such as legal factors (e.g. the need for additional security measures after 9/11).

- Lack of control over individuals who are in a position authorise changes without following due process.

- The contractor is very persuasive and psychologically gains and upper hand with the customer becoming reluctant to say no.

Avoiding Variations

It is essential that a process for managing any change to the scope of a contract is in place to ensure that any such variation is actually valid and required by the customer.

Failure to have such a process can lead to "scope creep", where the content of a contract keeps increasing without any real effective control.

Therefore there is a need for a "Change Control" process, which ensures that there is rigorous assessment of any potential variations. Whilst there is no absolutely correct model, a Change Control process would expect to cover the following:

- Is it a genuine variation or is it already in the defined scope?

- Is the change really necessary and something that will provide real benefit to the customer or is it just a "nice to have"?

- Has work already started on the variation without proper approval?

- Has a request for a variation been formally proposed either by the customer or the contractor?

- Has the change been approved by all relevant parties in the customer's organisation?

- Is the cost known or is an estimate available?

- Has the impact of the change on cost, programme, quality and health, safety and environment been assessed?

- Have mitigations for negative impacts of the variation been proposed?

Controlling Variations

Despite carrying out the actions above, which can help in avoiding variations, in some case they will be inevitable and to ensure proper management within the bounds of the contract, a formal process should be followed:

- The contractor (or a stakeholder of the customer) proposes a change to the scope of the contract and supplies a quotation giving the price and any potential effects on time, quality etc.

- The Contract Manager carries out an initial assessment as to whether the change:
  - Is already included in the contract specification.
  - Is actually outside the bounds of the contract specification and could be more appropriately served by letting a separate contract.

- Is actually required by the customer and is not just "a nice to have".
- Has a price that is affordable and effects on time and quality that can be borne without compromising the success of the original contract.

- If the variation is potentially valid, the price should be assessed for its reasonableness using:
  - Analogous rates within the contract (e.g. labour rates and material costs).
  - Prices from previous contracts.
  - Benchmarked costs from published sources such as trade publications.
  - Cost analysis by quantity surveyors, cost engineers and accountants.
  - Analysis of overhead and profit margins against those being generally earned by the contractor across other contracts (e.g. through examination of the report and accounts).

- The results of the assessment should be subject to the customer's change control process, which could be subject to certain thresholds of approval depending on the value and risk of the variation and/or the overall contract. This might start with the Contract Manager having the right of approval up to a certain level, then submission to more senior personnel, leading to approval by a Change Control Board, which may be made up from, amongst others, senior representatives from the commercial, finance and technical functions.

- Once approved, a formal variation instruction/order can be issued and the contractor can then undertake the work.

Consequences of Variations

Marsh states that "Variations may not be unfairly described as the cancer of contracting." – *PDV Marsh, Contracting for Engineering and Construction Projects.*

  We have to accept, where variations have been agreed, there will be consequences such as:

-     Increases in the final outturn cost of the contract.

-     Delays to completion.

-     Potential rework for changes to the specification of work that has already been completed.

-     Failure to meet required quality standards.

-     Disruption to agreed programmes of work.

-     The need to compress timings of some phases.

-     Cancellation/amendment of orders already placed on subcontractors.

-     A poor reputation gained for both the customer and contractor for contract management.

Claims

Reason for Claims

We have established earlier that a claim arises through additional costs incurred by the contractor outside his reasonable control. The range of issues against which contractors may claim is quite substantial, including in some cases down to the cost of drawing up the claim itself. It must be emphasised that the right to submit a claim depends on what is actually defined as allowable in the conditions of contract. The following is list of what is sometimes termed potential sources of a claim.

- Inability to gain access to say a site or building in order to commence work in accordance with the contract programme.

- Customer not making free issue materials or services available in accordance with the contract programme.

- Customer instructing changes in working pattern or working method that were not specified in the original contract leading to a loss of productivity.

- Drawing or specifications supplied by the customer containing mistakes, omissions, ambiguity or even contradictions.

- Delays in approval of documents or drawings submitted by the contractor.

- Delays affecting the contractor caused by third party contractors working for the customer.

- Costs associated with an extension of time granted to the contractor.

- External factors beyond the contractor's reasonable control such as exceptional weather, earthquake, national strikes, war etc.

- Additional financing costs caused by delays in receiving payments or release of retentions.

Avoiding Claims

Claims can be avoided by ensuring proper control of the contract through:

- Having clear and unambiguous conditions of contract.

- Having effective risk management to anticipate, reduce or eliminate potential sources of claims, before they happen.

- Ensuring a good relationship with the contractor is maintained.

- Having good management of the contract programme to ensure progress towards key milestones and activities on the critical path are fully monitored.

- Keeping detailed records in order to be able challenge any potentially incorrect statements made by the contractor.

On Receipt of a Claim

Before the value and terms of any claim are agreed, the following should be carried out:

- Ensure that the claim is in accordance with the provisions of the conditions of contract, defining the actual clause under which the claim is being submitted.

- Do not dismiss a claim, because it is believed that the contractor is being difficult or that it might be expensive.

- Ensure that the claim is being submitted in the format defined in the contract.

- Check if the claim been submitted within any time constraints in the conditions of contract.

- Check that substantiation of the claim, such that:
  - It is based on factual and verifiable evidence. For instance if it is based on delayed access by the customer, was that wholly the customer's responsibility?
  - Additional costs incurred as a direct result of the issue on which the claim is based and not any failure to control costs by the contractor. Claims based on costs less receipts can be used to hide the contractor's inefficiency.
  - The actual costs incurred excluding profit and overheads, unless the contract specifically allows for this. This would mean that claims should not be paid at tender rates nor should they based on vague percentages or cost allocations.
  - It is clear the contractor has made every attempt to mitigate the cost of claim, for example by rescheduling work, allowing labour that would be idle to carry out other tasks required by the contract.

- Agree a value for the claim and ensure that the contract price is duly amended.

Consequences of Claims

These will be similar to those listed for variations above. Once again, it is the effect on price, time and quality that is paramount.

Chapter Summary

In this chapter, we have examined the issue of changes to contracts and their consequences. In particular:

- The differences between variations and claims. A variation arises from a change in the scope of the contract; a claim from an increase in contractor's costs through actions of the customer or a third party, where such allowance is defined in the contract.

- Variations can lead to unfavourable changes in cost, time and quality and where there occur, should be managed through a change control process.

- Claims can also lead to unfavourable changes in cost, time and quality and where there occur, should be thoroughly assessed for validity and cost.

Case Study

Holiday Hotels is a large international chain of hotels, with headquarters in the UK. Recently the company let a large contract for the redecoration of its offices in Dublin. The contract was let to a small local company, Dublin Decorators Ltd.

The contract was let on the basis of the lowest price tendered. Within a few weeks of the works commencing the Contract Manager receives a call from the Office Supervisor. An accident has occurred on site. One of the painters has fallen from his ladder and injured his arm. The Contract Manager then receives a call from ABC Painters Ltd, demanding the insurance details of the company, as they wish to make a claim against the Company. ABC Painters is a very small firm and has forgot to renewed its own employee liability insurance cover.

The contract manager has never heard of ABC Painters and is informed by their owner that his company has been sub-contracted by Dublin Decorators to undertake a major proportion of the works. He also takes the opportunity to make the contract manager aware that all his outstanding invoices to Dublin Decorators remain, as yet, unpaid. The contract manager reviews the contract file and can find no record of any safety plan being submitted by Dublin Decorators regarding painting works.

Next day the Hotel Manager received a call from the local paper. A reporter from the Dublin Times is requesting clarification regarding the issue of Holiday Hotels trying to drive a small local company (ABC Painters Ltd) out of business, by not settling its invoices. The Hotel manager makes a rather brief call to the contracts manager, demanding an explanation. Later that same day the CEO of Holiday Hotels receives a call from the Managing Director of Omega Contractors. He is demanding to know why the recent re decoration contract awarded to Dublin Decorators (his local competitor) and why was he not invited to tender, given that his company is on the approved bidders list.

Task

As the Head of Contracts what would you do now?

10 Legal Aspects Concerning Management of the Contract

Introduction

There is rightly a great concentration on ensuring that contracts comply with law and are also robust against potential legal challenge. This is a key issue for pre-award of the contract and a detailed analysis is available in Chapter 14 of "Practical Procurement" by R J Carter and S K Kirby. This particular chapter aims merely at an overview of some of the practical steps needed to comply with legislation, whilst the contract is running. This is not an academic treatise and does not deal with case law and neither should it any way be deemed to constitute legal advice.

Late Payment of Commercial Debts (Interest) Act (1998)

Quite simply, this act gives contractors the statutory right to claim interest where a customer has made a late payment. The definition of late is significant. The Act does not prescribe or imply a mandated payment period into contracts. These can be freely negotiated as say 10, 30 or 90 days, though it does include a fallback position. When the contract is silent, the default period is 30 days and there is also potential for the courts to strike out excessive or unfair payment terms. Lateness is therefore defined as payment outside of the agreed period in the contract.

The key feature of the Act is a statutory right for the contractor to claim interest at a rate of 8% above the Bank of England base rate, plus any reasonable debt recovery costs. This is designed to be a remedy, which does not require a court ruling, as well as being punitive, since 8% above base rate should be above what a normal business would have to pay for approved overdraft facilities.

Customers need to be aware of this as any delay that they have caused (through failing to sign off a valid invoice) or on his behalf by the Accounts Payable function (though failing to make payment) could lead to increased cost, a worsening relationship with the Contractor as well as gaining a poor public reputation. In the long run, contractors become aware of bad payers and will include extra contingency in their tendered prices to cover such financing costs.

Changes to the Contract by Performance

It is a general legal principle that a legally binding contract that has been freely entered into by both parties can only be amended with the agreement of both parties. For a written contract, this would normally be through an agreed change control process and any such amendments would be signed onto by both parties. However just as there is a potential for creating a contract by performance, it can also be amended in this way. Examples might include:

- The contractor carrying out work outside of the scope of the contract and this being signed of and paid for, despite no verbal or written agreement being made to this change.

- Customer's staff other than the Contract Manager instructing the contractor to carry out work and not being countermanded by him.

- A service contract reaches its completion date without any formal renewal, but the contractor continues working and neither the customer's Contract Manager nor any other of the customer's staff prevents him.

The customer must make it clear in the contract that only the Contract Manager or his nominated representatives can make any changes to the contract or give additional instructions. Just as importantly, he and his colleagues must follow these rules as closely as he would expect the contractor to.

Appointment and Management of Sub-Contractors

There is often controversy over the use of sub-contractors, with an unwarranted feeling that sub-contracting is a bad thing and is used as a way of reducing cost, by employing cheaper, low quality labour and materials. Whilst this can happen, one should be aware of the other key issues.

Most importantly, the main contractor is wholly responsible for the performance of sub-contractors, specifically nominated by him. Thus if the sub-contractor fails in meeting an obligation, which causes the main contractor to fail to meet his obligations, then it is wholly the main contractor's responsibility. The customer seeks redress from him and not the sub-contractor. This principle is based on "privity of contract" and applies irrespective of whether such a clause exists in the contract.

The Contracts (Rights of Third Parties) Act (2000) has amended this principle slightly in that third parties now have the right to enforce rights in contracts to which they are not party if the contract states:

- The intention to do so or;

- The contract term purports to confer a benefit on the person. Such a third party must be identified in the contract though not necessarily by name. It is sufficient to nominate a description such as sub-contractors, the Engineer etc.

Despite not being in direct contract with a sub-contractor, the customer still needs to maintain an element of control through ensuring that:

- The contractor declares the names, scope and value of work carried out by the sub-contractor in the contract.

- The contract has a clause requiring the contractor to seek permission from the customer, before changing or appointing a new sub-contractor, as well as ensuring that it is enforced.

- A watching brief is kept on the performance of sub-contractors without actually interfering in the day-to-day supervision and referring any issue via the main contractor.

Letters of Intent

A Letter of Intent is simply a communication from the customer to the contractor stating that he intends to place a contract with him at some point in the future. It is often used where:

- Contract negotiations are still continuing, but there is a requirement to commence work urgently in order to be able to meet a key milestone or completion date.

- There is a need for the contractor to commence ordering long lead time materials.

- There is an urgent requirement, for which there is no time to engage in a normal tendering process.

- The organisation's internal contract awarding processes are so lengthy, that this is seen as a useful short-cut.

Letters of Intent, though seemingly a quick mechanism to commence work are fraught with danger in that they fall into a very grey area, as to whether a legally binding contract has been created. If they are vague, they may allow excessive freedom for the contractor to start incurring costs and if they are too detailed, a court may infer that a legally binding contract exists, as it may decide that was the intention of both parties all along. Even if a contract does not exist, the contractor will probably be entitled to payment under the principle of "quantum meruit" (as much as is deserved or merited). This allows the contractor to claim a reasonable amount for work carried out in accordance with the Letter of Intent and may be deemed by a higher amount, than would have been agreed through competition and any subsequent negotiations.

If, despite all the above, a Letter of Intent is required, it should contain the at least the following (better still, be avoided!):

- A schedule and programme of the work to be carried out.

- A limit of liability which defines the maximum value of cost that can be incurred and charged by the contractor.

- How payment will be made.

- A time limit stating when the Letter of Intent will cease.

A formal contract cancelling the Letter of Intent should be put in place as soon as possible. It has been known for major construction work to have been carried out, solely on the basis of a Letter of Intent.

A Letter of Intent should be distinguished from a **Letter of Comfort**, which is often used by a parent company to state that it will honour any contractual obligations not met by a subsidiary. These have doubtful legal enforceability and a more formally drawn up agreement in the form of a Parent Company Agreement would be more appropriate. This then creates a formal, legally contractual obligation on the parent company.

Rights under Consumer Protection Legislation

In the event that the Contractor is not performing his obligations under the contract, the contract itself will normally contain remedies for such issues as poor quality or delay. In their absence, legislation is in place to protect the customer and this is covered in detail in Chapter 14 of "Practical Procurement" by R J Carter and S K Kirby.

The key issue is whether the contractor has been able to exclude the customer's rights in the conditions of contract through an exclusion or limitation of liability clause. Such clauses could be deemed unreasonable under the Unfair Contract Terms Act (1977), which will depend on the context and the relative strengths of the parties. Thus, the customer may, if he feel has suffered from an exclusion clause, believe that it is unreasonable and refer to the court for a judgement. A example might be where the contractor in very strong negotiating position (through size or monopoly power) imposes a "reasonable endeavours" clause on the quality of an item, which may mean there is no guarantee that it will either be of satisfactory quality or be fit for purpose (i.e. an exclusion of rights under the Sale of Goods Act). Should the contractor try to impose this condition, the customer may have a case for it to be declared "unreasonable".

Related to the above is the concept of **Misrepresentation**. If a false statement of fact has induced the customer into entering a contract, this is deemed as misrepresentation. An example is the purchase of a car, where the mileage has been falsified or "clocked" to induce the purchaser to believe that it has had a lower usage that it has in reality. The customer may then have the right to claim damages or terminate the contract depending on the circumstances.

Health and Safety Legislation

We may believe that the reason that we need to comply with the key piece of legislation (i.e. Health and Safety at Work etc Act (1974)) is to avoid being prosecuted. However, it self-evident that we do not we do not wish to cause any injury to ourselves and that we feel a moral responsibility to others, both to those we know and to those we have never met. We would therefore not wish to work with a contractor who could cause us or others any harm.

There will also be economic consequences which go beyond the suffering of the individuals concerned such as:

- Compensation.

- Fines.

- Fees for legal and technical advice.

- Additional costs to cover individuals off work.

- Production shutdown.

- Loss of custom.

- Loss or reputation.

It may be tempting to believe that a customer has no responsibility for the actions of contractors and sub-contractors working on his premises However Section 3 (1) of the Health and Safety at Work Act etc. is very clear in this respect.

"It shall be the duty of every employer to conduct his undertaking in such a way as to ensure, so far as is reasonably practicable, that persons not in his employment who may be affected thereby are not thereby exposed to risks to their health or safety".

Customers therefore have a duty to individuals working as contractors or sub-contractors and therefore need to ensure that:

- They have the ability and the resources to manage the health and safety risk.

- The scope of work is written in a manner which will minimise risk.

- Only competent contractors are engage to carry out the work.

- A safe system of work is in place for the contractor to carry out the works.

- Adequate control and supervision is in place to ensure that all the arrangements put in place actually happen.

More detailed guidance is available from the Health and Safety Executive.

Contract Termination

A termination of a contract will occur when both of the parties to the contract are in some way released from their obligations. This can occur in the following ways:

- **Performance** – Both parties have completed all their obligations under the contract satisfactorily and thereby the contract comes to a natural end.

- **Agreement** – Both parties mutually agree not to continue with the performance of the contract.

- **Breach** – If one of the parties breaches a condition of the contract (i.e. one that goes to the heart of its performance), the other therefore has the right to terminate and claim damages.

- **Termination for Convenience** – Where a clause is expressly included in the contract, allowing a party (usually the customer) to terminate the contract, without breach having taken place. Normally, the contractor will be entitled to all reasonable costs incurred up to the point of termination.

- **Break** – there may be a provision in a contract, whereby at a specific date, either part may decide not to continue with the contract, normally on giving of due notice e.g. for property leases.

- **Frustration** – a contract becomes discharged because it is become impossible or illegal to perform due to unforeseen circumstances such as war, fire and Act of God. It is often written into a contract in the form of a "force majeure" clause, which defines such circumstances.

Chapter Summary

In this chapter, we have covered the following legal issues which may impact on contract management:
- Late Payment of Commercial Debts (Interest) Act.

- Changes to the Contract by Performance.

- Appointment and Management of Sub-Contractors.

- Letters of Intent.

- Rights under Consumer Protection Legislation.

- Health and Safety Legislation.

- Contract Termination.

It is emphasised that this chapter constitutes general guidance only and individuals should take legal advice for specific cases.

Case Study

Torch Ltd are a group of engineering consultants, based in London. The company has recently secured a contract for the supply of a team of consultants to assist in the development of a technical scope of work for the new gas plant turnkey contract for Allied Oil and Gas plc. Part of the contract includes attending a series of meetings with the key stakeholders at the various sites around the UK. These are considered to be very important events.

A meeting is planned for the 15th July at 10am. Two consultants from Torch are due to attend. By chance, this meeting will also be attended by the CEO of Allied – Peter Pan. Due to a family crisis, one consultant does not make the meeting and the other one is late by one hour, due to local traffic. Peter is very angry at this unprofessional behaviour and informs the consultants that he intends to terminate the whole contract, with immediate effect and will make a claim for his wasted time, given that this critical event has not been properly resourced by Torch.

Task

Advise the consultants regarding the issue of breach of warranty and condition.

11 Dispute Resolution and Alternative Dispute Resolution

Introduction

However well set-up and managed a contract might be during its lifetime, disputes can still occur between contracts officer and contractor. Whilst steps should always be taken to minimise disputes through effective contract management, if and when they do occur it is useful to be aware of possible methods of resolving them. These methods are as follows:

Negotiation: the vast majority of claims and disputes can be settled by amicable negotiation leading to an agreement. This is the quickest and least costly method of settling disputes and is usually the preferred first course of action should a dispute with a contractor arise.

Mediation: this is a form of alternative dispute resolution (ADR) and is a way of resolving disputes between two parties. A third party, the mediator, assists the parties to negotiate their own settlement.

Adjudication: this is a process of expert determination where an expert is appointed by agreement between the parties, either generally or to decide a particular issue.

Arbitration: again, this is a form of expert determination but is more formal than adjudication.

Litigation: this is the term used to describe dispute resolution in the courts. It tends to be a time-consuming, costly and complex process, and is often used only as a last resort.

Dispute Resolution

Negotiation

Negotiation has been mentioned above as the quickest and least costly method of dispute resolution. There is nothing really to add to that except to say that, generally, it is the method that contracts officers should try to adopt first. Apart from the speed and low cost, negotiation usually has the benefit of allowing contracts officer and contractor to maintain a good relationship. This is usually not true of other methods of dispute resolution. Unfortunately, there is always the possibility that negotiation will not succeed in resolving a dispute and in this situation, one of the other methods needs to be considered. We will now examine each of these in order of cost, speed and easiness of application.

Mediation

Here, a third party, known as the mediator, assists the parties to negotiate their own settlement: a process known as facilitative mediation. In some cases, where both parties agree, mediators may express a view on what might be a fair or reasonable settlement: a process known as evaluative mediation. Mediation improves stalled negotiations because it is assisted and guided by the mediator.

Mediation has a structure, timetable and dynamics that 'ordinary' negotiation lacks. The process is private and confidential but the presence of a mediator is the key distinguishing feature of the process.

Mediators use various techniques to open or improve dialogue between the parties in dispute, aiming to help the parties reach an agreement on the disputed matter. Here, much depends on the mediator's skill and training and the mediator must be wholly impartial with respect to the outcome. However, they do have control over the process and pace of the negotiations. The mediator's duty and expertise lies in assisting the parties in exploring the range of settlement options and coming to a mutually acceptable outcome.

The mediator cannot compel either party to resolve the dispute in any given way because the parties retain absolute control over the outcome. Mediators meet jointly and privately with all parties in order to gain a thorough understanding of the parties' needs and interests. Because the process is confidential, parties are able to test their perception of the facts and the law with the assistance of an unbiased third party. Even in those cases where resolution is not achieved, mediation is still beneficial because it serves to streamline the issues in dispute.

Mediation is most appropriate when an ongoing business relationship is involved. It is in no-one's best interest to subject a business relationship to the adversarial and divisive system of litigation if the parties wish to conduct business together in the future. Mediation enjoys a very high rate of success especially when the parties have mutual interests that can be satisfied by a resolution of the dispute. Such interests could include the progress and completion of a contract.

Mediation is best entered into early in the life of a dispute before parties have committed to hard-and-fast positions, and before anger, hostility and the expenditure of large sums of time and money have poisoned the atmosphere. That is the point in time when a neutral, objective and impartial third party may assist the parties in achieving results which can be imaginative, inventive, and not necessarily based on a monetary settlement. It is this ability to craft results which meet the parties' underlying interests and overall objectives that is unique to mediation and one of its many significant benefits.

Mediation can be done quickly and in a cost-effective manner. The process can be started within days or weeks and, because it is a somewhat informal process, preparation time can be kept to a minimum and the parties usually split the costs equally. Unlike litigation, the process of mediation is one that allows the direct participation of those actually involved in the dispute (as well as their lawyers), thus creating the likelihood of more satisfactory and durable settlements.

It is for all of the above reasons that mediation is sometimes referred to colloquially as 'negotiation under the eye of a referee'. However, if a mutually acceptable resolution cannot be achieved, resolution by some other process will be required.

Adjudication

This involves the reference of a dispute to an independent third party who reaches a formal decision that acts as an imposed resolution of the dispute. This is a process of expert determination where the expert is appointed by agreement between the parties, either generally or to decide a particular issue. Provided the expert keeps within the terms of the appointment and shows no bias, there is no restriction on the way a decision can be reached.

Adjudication is less formal, and generally quicker and less costly than arbitration and litigation. If the contract provides for the expert determination to be final and binding, in other words, if both parties agree, a court will not interfere with the decision reached. If the contract has no such provision, however and adjudication does not achieve final settlement of a dispute, either of the parties has the right to have the same dispute heard afresh in court (or where the contract specifies arbitration, in arbitration proceedings). Nevertheless, the majority of adjudication decisions are accepted by the parties as the final result.

Adjudication can be used at any time. For example, provided the parties have a contractual relationship it can be used to decide contractual disputes. Once a dispute has arisen between the parties either party may seek adjudication and will then select an adjudicator. Once the adjudicator has made their decision, the other party must comply with it: if they do not, a court hearing to compel compliance can usually be obtained in a matter of days.

Adjudication is designed to be a simple process to enable disputes to be resolved inexpensively and quickly. In many cases it will not be necessary for the complainant to incur the cost of obtaining professional assistance from lawyers, claims consultants, or other specialists. Contracts officers may be able to seek assistance from their trade association or professional body. However, proper preparation and presentation of a written case to the adjudicator may be a critical factor in the success or failure of the contracts officer's arguments.

The adjudicator usually only has a short time, often only two or three weeks, in which to consider the arguments put forward by both parties before reaching their decision. Where the facts of a dispute are straightforward and the referring party wishes the adjudicator to make a decision about how much should be paid and to whom, preparation of the case can probably be done without professional assistance.

Where the case involves complicated technical or legal issues, however, it may be necessary to seek professional help and if this is the case, it is recommended to seek it at the earliest opportunity, preferably before the adjudication process is started.

The adjudication process

Adjudication usually follows the following process:

- **Notice of adjudication:** Once satisfied that there is a dispute, the complainant can initiate adjudication by submitting a written notice of adjudication to the other party. The notice must be given to the other party (or where the contract is between more than two parties to every party to the contract). The notice must contain the following details:

- Nature and brief description of the dispute and the parties involved.
- When and where the dispute arose.
- The nature of the redress being sought.
- Names and addresses of the parties to the contract.

The notice of adjudication is an important document – it defines what matters the adjudicator has to decide. It is vital that notice of adjudication is comprehensive and covers every aspect of the dispute. It should contain the following elements:

- **A description of the dispute** – care should be taken because an imprecise description could result in a challenge to any decision an adjudicator makes.
- **Details of how the dispute has arisen** – this will be required mainly to show that there actually is a 'dispute' to refer to adjudication.
- **The decision that the adjudicator is required to make and the remedy or remedies sought** – these will need to be specific about the remedies required and will either be a declaration of principle and/or an order for the payment of money. If the adjudicator is required to make an order that the contracts officer should be paid money, the contracts officer's notice must clearly ask the adjudicator to do so. The adjudicator's decision may be only partially (and not entirely) in the contracts officer's favour. For this reason, it should be specified that the adjudicator may make such other decision as they sees fit.
- The **names and addresses of the parties involved** in the dispute – everything required should be covered in the notice.

- **Appointment of adjudicator:** All adjudicators must be impartial and should not unfairly regard with favour or disfavour the case of one of the parties, nor should there be any appearance that the adjudicator might do so. The original contract may name an adjudicator, a panel of adjudicators or an Adjudicator Nominating Body. If it does, then we must use the named person or body. If it does not, or if the person named declines to act and the contract does not provide for a substitute, then an Adjudicator Nominating Body may be approached to select a person to act. As the name suggests, Adjudicator Nominating Bodies are organisations that have set themselves up to nominate adjudicators. A number of professional bodies and trade associations have set up Adjudicator Nominating Bodies If there is a choice as to which Adjudicator Nominating Body to use, it is recommended that the choice should be based on the skills envisaged that the adjudicator should possess to decide the dispute.

- **Referral notice:** The next step is for the complainant to send a referral notice to both the adjudicator and the other party (all documents must be copied to the other party as well as to the adjudicator). The period for the decision starts on the date when the adjudicator receives the referral notice. This is the document which contains all the information that the adjudicator should consider. It should:
  - Be consistent with the notice of adjudication.
  - Explain the nature of the dispute and how it arose
  - Detail the facts that are relied upon.
  - Provide the documentary evidence to support those facts.
  - Provide sufficient details of the contract to show that there is a contractual right to the remedy sought.
  - List the decisions that we require the adjudicator to make.

It should not include evidence (for example, an expert's report or test results) that the other side has not seen before; this could be challenged and possibly stop the adjudicator's decision being enforced.

The notice should be a clear statement of the referring party's case. It is unwise to rely solely on providing the adjudicator with correspondence about the dispute, since this will normally assume many of the facts relating to the dispute because they are well known to both writer and receiver, while the facts will be unknown to the adjudicator. The referral notice is therefore best written as a narrative, detailing in chronological order the events as they occurred starting with the formation of the contract, the parties, its aim and how it came into being. This should be followed by a description of the events leading up to the dispute, cross-referenced to documentary evidence attached in appropriate appendices.

The differences and arguments between the parties should be explained, in chronological order and the party referring the matter to adjudication should endeavour to address the arguments of their opponent and explain why these are considered to be wrong.

The referring party must prove their case to the adjudicator. It is likely that where there is a direct clash of assertions, with the referring party alleging one thing and the other party saying the opposite, then in the absence of any other evidence, the referring party will lose because the adjudicator considers that they have not adequately demonstrated their case. Evidence is, generally, the information that can be provided, documentary or otherwise (for instance, samples), which backs up the referring party's case.

- **Challenging the adjudicator's appointment:** There may be circumstances when one of the parties feels that the adjudicator has no jurisdiction (authority) because, for example, the referring party has sought to appoint an adjudicator in contravention of the procedure set out in the contract; or they do not think that there is a dispute.

If there is any doubt about the adjudicator's authority to act, it is suggested that legal advice be sought. Again, this should be done at an early stage, before taking any other steps. After taking advice, if it is thought to be appropriate, the referring party should write to the adjudicator, with a copy to the other party, setting out clearly the reasons for saying that the adjudicator does not have jurisdiction in the dispute. It is possible that the adjudicator will agree with this statement.

- **What does the adjudicator do next?** The adjudicator has to carry out their duties in accordance with the terms of the contract and make a decision in accordance with the law applicable to the contract. The adjudicator has to act impartially and avoid incurring unnecessary expense but subject to these considerations and the provisions of the adjudication procedure, has a very free hand as to how the adjudication is run.

- **What will actually happen?** The adjudicator should take the initiative in ascertaining the facts and the law necessary to reach a decision, and it is up to the adjudicator to decide on the procedure to be followed. In particular, the adjudicator should:
    - Request any party to the contract to supply any documents reasonably required, including further written statements.
    - Decide what language should be used (in international cases), including whether translations are needed.
    - Decide whether to meet parties and their representatives.

- Impose deadlines or limits to the length of documents or oral representations.
- Issue other directions for the conduct of the adjudication.

- **Will there be a formal hearing?** It is up to the adjudicator to decide whether to hold a hearing or not (this will depend on what the adjudicator feels is necessary in wer case). If there is a hearing, the adjudicator will also decide how formal it is to be: most will be relatively informal but it will be up to the parties to decide whether they want legal representation or not.

- **What can be expected from an adjudicator's decision?** The adjudicator's decision may be an order for the payment of money from one party to the other or it may relate to a disputed fact or technical matter (for example, whether the workmanship is to the right standard or what the specification means). The adjudicator may also decide that any of the parties to the dispute is liable to make a payment under the contract and decide when that payment is due and the final date for payment. The adjudicator also has power to award interest (either simple or compound) on outstanding payments.
  Adjudicators have power to consider any type of dispute or difference arising under the contract but they may not decide issues that have not been referred (that is, adjudicators are restricted to the dispute referred to in the notice of adjudication) and may only make the decision sought in the referral notice.

- **Will the adjudicator provide written reasons?** It depends on the terms of the adjudication procedure: If the referring party wants the adjudicator to provide reasons therefore, they should request them at the earliest opportunity. Reasons help the parties to understand the decision and may assist in determining a future course of action.

- **Who pays the adjudicator's costs?** This depends upon the terms of the adjudication procedure. It is for the adjudicator to decide who should pay their costs as part of the decision. Often, the adjudicator will decide that the party that is losing overall must pay costs. However, this is not always the case and they may take into account matters such as how each party has behaved, and whether each party has won on some issues. On the other hand, whatever the outcome of the decision, the adjudicator may simply apportion the fees equally between the parties. If the adjudicator has obtained expert advice, provided that they have notified the parties first, they are entitled to appoint experts, assessors or legal advisers as required and the costs of any such external advice will form part of the adjudicator's costs.

- **What happens if the decision is in the complainant's favour but the other party is refusing to comply?** If a party does not comply with an adjudicator's decision, the other party can enforce that decision by going to court although legal advice will usually need to be obtained as well as representation to do this.

- **What happens if the referring party does not agree with the adjudicator's decision?** There is very clear law indicating that, generally, the courts will enforce adjudication decisions without enquiring as to their correctness. The exceptions are as follows:
    - Jurisdiction: That is, where the adjudicator has acted without having the authority to act or to make the decision that has been made. Examples are where

the adjudicator decides something that they were not asked to decide, or has not done what was asked of them; where the adjudicator has been appointed wrongly; and where there was no dispute in the first place.

- Natural justice: That is, where the adjudicator has not acted in accordance with procedural fairness in the conduct of the adjudication. There are two parts to natural justice: the adjudicator must be impartial and must allow each party the opportunity to make its case.

Arbitration

Arbitration can be defined as a voluntary judicial process to ascertain, declare and enforce the respective rights and obligations of the parties to a contract. While there may be notional pleadings and a discovery stage to arbitration, they are not as formal as those in litigation. Arbitration is the private equivalent of the public system of litigation in the courts. Like litigation, it involves the submission of a dispute to or resolution by an arbitrator rather than a judge. The arbitrator can be chosen (unlike a judge) but the parties have to pay for both the arbitrator's time and the hire of any venue for the arbitration hearing.

Arbitration differs from litigation as follows:

- The parties are free to agree their own procedures for the conduct of arbitration. In practice, for example, arbitration in the construction industry has tended to adopt similar procedures to litigation although this is not necessary.

- An arbitrator is empowered to make orders compelling compliance with directions although such orders can only be enforced by an order of a court.

- An arbitrator, like a judge may make an award of costs in favour of the successful party.

- An arbitrator, unlike a judge, can be chosen from any given field and therefore is likely to be chosen for their expertise and knowledge of the subject matter causing the dispute. This may or may not be an advantage: it can at least be said of a judge that their mind is not cluttered with any preconceived technical notions and they are better qualified to determine such issues as credibility and weight of evidence.

- Privacy can be an advantage of arbitration, but as all decisions are private, there is no established case law to refer to and thus there can be a lack of predictability in using such a forum.

- If arbitration is chosen as a means to resolve a dispute, it will be the sole arbiter of fact, and appeal will lie only on points of law to the Court. Contract clauses which make arbitration final and binding will not oust the Court's jurisdiction to review on appeal questions of law.

Issues that need to be considered following receipt of the Arbitration notice might be:

- Would the party in receipt of the notice prefer to seek a negotiated settlement of the dispute? The prospects of a negotiated settlement may depend on the parties' actual or perceived bargaining positions.

- What are the true merits of the parties' respective positions? To the extent that this position is not presently clear, what further investigation needs to be carried out, and by whom?

- If the arbitration is to proceed, or if there remains a risk that it may proceed, who would be the parties' choice of an arbitrator? Typical contract conditions might state that, if the parties cannot agree on an arbitrator within 14 days of the giving of notice to concur in the appointment of an arbitrator, the party implementing the procedure has the choice of appointing the arbitrator.

Timescales and cost of arbitration

It is very difficult to give a meaningful timescale or estimate of the cost of arbitrating a dispute but it is quite likely that any arbitration would involve a prolonged hearing and would therefore be expensive to resolve.

The following factors may have an important effect on the timescale and cost:

- The willingness of both parties to resolve the dispute quickly.

- The availability of the chosen arbitrator and any expert witnesses or witnesses of fact.

- The ability of the arbitrator to control the pace of the proceedings.

- Whether there are any preliminary issues that can be decided separately that, once resolved, may greatly simplify the resolution of the remaining issues.

Stages in the Arbitration process

The following are the usual stages in the arbitration process in chronological order:

- Notice of Arbitration passed from the party bringing the complaint to the other party.

- Appointment of the Arbitrator.

- Points of defence (and counterclaim) made by the recipient of the complaint.

- Exchange of Witness Statements between the parties: the arbitrator should have sight of these).

- 'Without Prejudice' meeting of expert witnesses or witnesses of fact.

- Exchange of above experts' reports.

- The actual Arbitration hearing.

- Award made by the arbitrator (this will have limited rights of appeal).

- Enforcement of the award and allocation of costs.

- Enforcement of Costs Order.

Arbitration is more formal than adjudication, and resembles litigation, although it will generally be less costly. It is a semi-judicial process, with evidence being heard by an impartial, neutral, arbitrator (or panel of three arbitrators) whose decision is final and enforceable in court. The hearing of evidence is an important distinction between arbitration and adjudication.

An independent arbitrator is usually chosen after the dispute arises, although not always. For example, an insurance policy usually contains a clause providing for this method of settling any disputes which may arise. Contracts officer and contractor may also agree on arbitration as a means of dispute resolution and insert a clause to this effect in the contract. The arbitrator is appointed to hear arguments presented by the parties. The type of arbitrator chosen will depend on the nature of the case. The arbitrator's main role is to try to effect a settlement between the parties rather than to impose a judgement as to who is right or wrong.

Arbitration may also involve aspects of law, because many arbitrators are experienced lawyers, whereas adjudication is more concerned with the facts of the dispute. Unlike the adjudicator, an arbitrator cannot be sued for negligence. If the parties to a contract are unable to settle a dispute by arbitration, then there is no alternative but to enter into litigation.

Arbitration is swift (generally concludes three to four months from inception), private and informal with relaxed rules of evidence. It may arise in different ways:

By contract – the parties may, by contract, include a clause in the contract agreeing to refer any dispute to an arbitrator. This person may be named in the contract: for example, almost all vehicle insurance policies have such a clause.

By ruling of a court – a judge may decide to refer a dispute to arbitration.

By statute – for example, under the Marine Insurance Act 1905, maritime disputes are to be settled by arbitration. London is an international arbitration centre, with 70-80% of all disputes being referred to it.

The Arbitration Act 1996 has significantly improved the procedures for arbitration and the most important points are:

• The parties can agree or the arbitration tribunal can decide on what procedures are to apply to the arbitration.

• The right of either party to appeal to the courts has been severely restricted.

- The powers of the court to support the arbitrator have been strengthened.

- If the parties so agree, the arbitrator can decide the dispute not in accordance with a system of law but according to equity and good faith.

- If there is an arbitration clause in the contract, then the dispute must be referred to arbitration unless the arbitration agreement cannot be performed. The court no longer has any discretion in the matter.

- The award of the arbitrator is enforceable in the same way as a judgement of the court.

Advantages of arbitration

The advantages of arbitration and why it is preferred to court action are:

- It avoids publicity – proceedings are held in private.

- Parties can select and stipulate the identity of the arbitrator. If the parties cannot agree on who is to be appointed, then the Arbitration Act (1996) gives the courts the power to do so.

- It is less formal than litigation – the informal atmosphere and straightforward procedure is often preferred by the parties involved.

- It is flexible – it avoids the rigidity sometimes imposed by the doctrine of judicial precedent that tends to govern the courtroom process.

- There is often greater specialist knowledge – more commercially aware staff are often involved.

- It is usually less expensive than litigation. The procedure is cheaper, although the costs of the arbitrator may be quite high and the time spent on arbitration is often less than on a civil litigation case in the Commercial Court. Discouraging legal representation potentially reduces the fees further.

- It is usually much quicker than litigation.

- An arbitrator's award may be enforced by the courts in the same way as a High Court judgement. Here, the courts allow the parties to settle their own disputes but, at the same time maintain a supervisory role.

- The proceedings can be held at the convenience of both parties.

Disadvantages of arbitration

Arbitration does have disadvantages, however, which are:

- Arbitrators are often not skilled in applying or interpreting the law although there is a trend towards arbitrators also being senior lawyers.

- There are no formal rules for arbitration and discretion can lead to inconsistent and unpredictable decisions.

- The parties might still end up in court even after the arbitration process if it has not been possible to reach a mutually-satisfactory agreement.

- Appeal is only possible on a point of law, not point of fact.

- When a non-lawyer is appointed as an arbitrator a dispute is much more likely to be resolved on the basis of a compromise than would be the case if it went to court. This is said to favour contractors who bring excessively over-valued claims, on specious grounds, in the hope of getting something, which they often do!

- The procedural rules are much weaker than those of courts and depend very much on cooperation between the parties. This may not be forthcoming if one party wants to delay. There is also some reliance on the strength of purpose of the arbitrator.

- If the dispute concerns a matter of law or construction/interpretation of contract terms, it is better dealt with in the courts where there is greater expertise in such matters.

- Unless an arbitrator is very experienced, they will not have the same capabilities as a judge in distinguishing between truthful and untruthful evidence.

It is worth mentioning that another form of arbitration is the small claims court.

Since 1973 there has been an arbitration service within the County Court via the small claims procedure. Registrars, who tend to be solicitors, hear cases; they listen mainly to debt cases up to £5 000.

In addition to the small claims court, or as an alternative to it, many consumer organisations operate forms of arbitration, but most are run by the various industry bodies such as ABTA (Association of British Travel Agents), which looks after arbitration in the travel industry.

A common benefit to mediation, adjudication and arbitration, known collectively as **'Alternative Dispute Resolution (ADR)'**, is that each is a private process. If the dispute involves competitive bidding practices, trade secrets, critical employment information, long-term corporate strategies or other sensitive information, such information can be kept in strict confidence and free from public scrutiny. Also, major processes of litigation can have much adverse publicity for both parties, which is avoided by ADR.

It is worth noting that arbitration is often used to resolve disputes of an international nature.

Litigation

Litigation is the process whereby disputes are settled by submitting them to the decision of a court of law and conducted in public. It is easy and tempting to suppose that every time we disagree with a contractor we take them to court. The fact is, however, that litigation is usually the last resort but may be the only course of action where the use of a consensual process is not provided for in the contract and cannot otherwise be agreed, hence the importance of planning when drafting a contract. Judgements are binding on parties subject to rights of appeal.

Litigation requires trial before a judge, and may well be a lengthy, drawn out and costly process so the parties often agree a settlement before the case comes to court. It is highly likely that the relationship will have broken down by this stage and will be irreparable. Litigation can also create much adverse publicity.

Under English law, cases between businesses are usually heard in the high court, often by a single judge, although the normal appeal process for a party not satisfied with the decision via the Court of Appeal, and finally the Supreme Court, applies.

Generally, there are three stages of litigation:

Pleadings: These are the written allegations setting out a plaintiff's (the aggrieved party) cause of action and claim for relief.

The Discovery process: Discovery is the process where the parties to an action disclose to each other all documents in their possession, custody or power relating to the matter in question.

With the exception of documents under solicitor-client privilege and those made in contemplation of litigation, all relevant documents are open to examination. During this process there will also be Examinations in Aid of Discovery, wherein potential witnesses to an action are examined under oath.

The main purpose of the Discovery process is to define the issues that will go to trial and also to test the strength of each party's case. After this process, the parties usually know where they stand, and as a result it is after discovery that most actions are settled.

The trial: This is the actual legal process that takes place in court.

Chapter Summary

In this chapter we have considered dispute resolution and the possible means of achieving this. These start with negotiation, being the easiest, quickest and cheapest means of dispute resolution and then proceed through:

Mediation: a means of dispute resolution using a third party who, in effect, acts as a 'referee' between the two parties during negotiation. This is a relatively quick and cheap method of dispute resolution.

Adjudication: a relatively informal means of dispute resolution involving selection and use of a third party who is usually an expert on the subject matter of the dispute rather than a legal expert. Adjudication is more formal than mediation but less formal than arbitration.

Arbitration: a more formal means of dispute resolution involving selection and use of a third party who is often a legal expert. Decisions reached in this manner are more often than not legally-binding but the process is more time-consuming and costly than adjudication.

Litigation: This is suing the other party in a court of law, a process that can be very time-consuming and expensive. Generally speaking, contracts officers will want to avoid this process and will attempt to resolve disputes using Alternative Dispute Resolution methods such as those listed above.

Case Study

Competent Technical Service Consultants Ltd are a UK based company, specialising in providing on site technical support and advise on how to improve production efficiency in the context of multi site catering operations. The company is very well respected in the market place and several of its more senior consultants are well know experts in the field, one has published a well know book entitled *"Catering Improvements"* everyone in the industry has a copy…

The company is contracted by the Ideal Catering Company (ICC) an international catering company, to provide on site support and advice. The contract has been awarded on a fixed day rate basis and bonus, plus economy air travel. The consultants are use to travelling business class and the fare difference is quite small, but ICC has insisted. Shortly after the contract had been awarded the team of consultants arrives on site to commence the work in the Middle East, where ICC has several major operations.

An inaugural meeting with Ali, the contract administrator, is scheduled for 10am on the first day, but Ali is delayed and does not arrive until 11.30. During the meeting with the consultants Ali makes it clear that he expects the team to meet their "contractual obligations" and that he will be monitoring their progress very closely. He also implies that his own team could have undertaken this work, but are too busy on more important work. During the meeting Ali is constantly answering calls on his mobile, many of which appear to be relating to trivial matters. Ali is keen for the improvements to benefit the local community; the consultants are more interested in achieving their targets to secure the bonus.

The consultancy team was meant to be headed up by Peter Jones, but he decided that he was too busy and has sent Ms Claudia Jordan in his place. At the meeting Claudia states that from her study of the results of previous studies, many mistakes have been made by Ali and his team (who are present at the meeting) and that poor leadership is a key issue. She states that she will be able to show them how to do much better in the future. She also points out that some food contracts seem to have been award to less than competent local contractors, at higher prices.

The consultants commence work the next day, but within a few weeks the project has come to complete stop. The consultants are complaining about a complete lack of co-operation from Ali and his team, while Ali sites arrogance on the part of the consultants. Both sides are threatening to take legal action.

Task

What has caused this contract to breakdown and how can this dispute can resolved?

12 Public Sector Contracting

Introduction

It is very easy to make snap judgements about managing contracts in the public sector. One the one hand, commentators will tell you that managing a contract requires exactly the same approach irrespective of whether it is in the private or public sector or in any country in the world – the principles are the same as is the required outcome – value for money. On the other hand, there is an equally strong argument that the public sector is so constrained by political agendas and bureaucracy that ultimately contract management must be carried out in a completely different manner than in the private sector.

There is an element of truth in both of these views as the reality is somewhere in between. This chapter will try to compare and contrast the similarities and differences in approach.

Key Difference Between Public and Private Sector Contracting

We should recognise that organisations in the public sector are ultimately accountable to the taxpayer, be they central or local, whilst in the private sector, the accountability is to the shareholders. We will now explore some of the key issues surrounding this principle.

What is the Public Sector?

The public sector is not just one single monolithic entity, but is a wide range of organisations with very different missions. We can include (with examples):

- Central Government (Ministry of Defence, Department for Work and Pensions.

- Local Government (County Councils, Unitary Authorities).

- Devolved Administrations (Scottish Parliament, Welsh Assembly).

- Quasi-autonomous non-governmental organisations (Highways Agency, National Audit Office).

- Public Corporations (BBC).

- Independent Trusts (as in the National Health Service).

- Voluntary and Community Organisations (VCOs) providing a public service, with taxpayer or voluntary funding (e.g. Local community groups or charities such as the Royal National Lifeboat Institution.

It should also be understood that across the world, there will be similar public sector organisations, which will also be ultimately accountable to their citizens. The actual legislation may be different in detail, but for example the USA also has a Freedom of Information Act; other countries may have clauses requiring them to give preference to contractors within their national boundaries or to use a minimum percentage of locally employed labour or individuals from ethnic minorities or disadvantaged citizens. In all cases, there will be additional constraints on public sector bodies, which are not apparent in the private sector.

Objectives

The private sector's ultimate objective is to make a profit for its shareholders/ owners and though there will of course be subsidiary objectives such as long-term growth, sustainability, increasing market share. In the public sector, the ultimate objective is to provide a service to the people of the nation, whilst obtaining the best value for money. In this sense, the contract manager needs to be more mindful of issues other than just the bottom line in cash terms such as:

- Improvements to society: e.g. increased longevity; better pupil: teacher ratios; better healthcare; reducing poverty.

- Improvements to the environment: e.g. reductions in Carbon Dioxide emissions; cleaner beaches; better public facilities.

An example is the concept of "Best Value" which is defined on the Local Government Improvement and Development website (www.idea.gov), as "each local authority has a duty to make arrangements to secure continuous improvement in the way in which its functions are exercised, having regard to a combination of economy, efficiency and effectiveness.

This improvement involves consideration of costs, making the most of money spent, and making sure that services meet the needs of communities and authorities' priorities." It is clear from this example that there is a necessary mix of value for money and service provision.

Public sector buyers must pay greater attention to the whole-life costs of construction projects to make savings of 20% The UK government has called for sweeping reforms in the way the public sector buys construction services to increase value for money. The report calls for a move away from concentrating on a price upfront in favour of more innovative strategies, reducing the number of players in the supply chain and increasing the focus on overall value of service.

Legal Compliance

A key difference between the private and public sectors is the issue of compliance with legislation, directly affecting public bodies.

The key piece of legislation is of course the Public Contract Regulations (2006), which lays down strict rules for advertising, shortlisting, evaluating and awarding contracts to ensure non-discrimination, equal treatment and transparency in public procurement across the European Union. This also applies to countries who are members of the European Economic Area such as Norway, Iceland and World Trade Organisation such as the USA, Japan. Once the contract is in place, it is easy to think that the issues surrounding this legislation have gone away and we can relax. There are however some issues that the contract manager must continue to consider:

- Any attempt to re-negotiate the terms and conditions or additions or deletions to the scope of the work, which materially alter the original intention of the contract might be seen, particularly by unsuccessful contractors as an attempt to avoid advertising the new requirement. Thus, if a contract was let for £1 million and a variation is used to add say another £4 million, this would almost be seen as a breach of the regulations.

- Extending the period of the contract, without having declared this as an option in the original advertisement, would also be seen as a breach. This is not uncommon, particularly when a contract is about to expire and not enough time has been allowed to put in place its replacement.

The other key piece of legislation is the Freedom of Information Act (2000) which gives rights of access to the public for information held by public authorities. In particular Section 43 of the Act sets out an exemption from this right if:

- The information requested is a trade secret.

- Release of the information is likely to prejudice the commercial interests of any person.

This is not however a blanket exemption. Unless the information constitutes a trade secret, such information can only be withheld if the public authority believes that the public interest in withholding the information outweighs the public interest in disclosing it. This is not a straightforward decision and responses to requests for information about a specific contract by other contractors and interested bodies would have to consider such issues as:

- Is the information useful to a competitor?

- Could its release damage the contractor financially or in reputation?

- Is there an issue of accountability for how the money has been spent?

Victoria Ross states in *Supply Management* that purchasing for a charity does not automatically exclude the need to conduct a formal procurement process, and usually a full OJEU process will be required. Grants or other contractual arrangements between public bodies and charities that do not involve the procurement of goods or services by the public body will not need a formal OJEU process, but some form of competition may be required.

Procedural Compliance

Where public money is being spent, a public sector organisation will want to be able to demonstrate that it has control over its expenditure process and displays full transparency and probity, in order to prevent fraud or general malpractice. In some cases, compliance may be seen as a higher priority than value for money, in view of the potential reputational consequences. Though the private sector may utilise these controls as well, it is more likely to be in a much less rigid manner.

- Formal tender opening may be used, where all bids received are sealed, opened at the same time, often by persons independent of the transaction.

- Delegations of authority are often in place, where the person authorised to make a legally binding commitment in the form of a purchase order, contract or variation has a maximum value placed upon that commitment. This will usually depend upon the person's grade, professional qualification or level of competence.

- A three-way segregation (or separation) of duties is also often in place. This generally requires that the following roles must all be carried out by different persons:
  - The person wanting the item or service (the budget holder or contract manager on his behalf) who specifies, manages and signs off satisfactory receipt or completion.
  - The person making the legal binding commitment (normally the procurement officer).
  - The person authorising the payment to be made (normally the finance officer in the Accounts Payable function).

  The reasoning behind this is:
  - Because there are three persons in involved in the transaction, the possibility of fraud is substantially reduced as there would need to be a high degree of collusion.
  - Each function can exert a degree of check and balance over the others. For example the finance officer will not pay an invoice, unless he is certain that the item or service has been received to the satisfaction of the contract manager and that the

payment will only be made in accordance with the terms and conditions of contract.

- In order to ensure that defined procedures are being followed, a governance process should be in place. This should consist of an independent review of such matters as change control, authorisation of work completed, by say another contract manager, a procurement officer, an internal auditor or an external consultant.

Perception

There will always be greater public and media interest in any contracting in the public sector rather than the private sector. Overspends on major public projects such as the Scottish Parliament, British Library attract a lot of attention from the public and politicians alike, though the oil spill at the Deepwater Horizon drilling rig in the Gulf of Mexico has also been high on the public agenda, notwithstanding that BP is a private company.

The contract manager will have to be mindful of a very large number of stakeholders, who have an interest and influence over the contract he is managing. The approach to these will be very different and the contract manager should have a stakeholder plan. In no particular order, the stakeholders can include:

- Elected representatives.
- Political advisers and consultants.
- Taxpayers.
- Public Relations and Communications Departments.
- Other departments.
- Regulatory or enforcement bodies.
- Members of the business community
- Trade Unions.
- Professional Bodies.
- Community and voluntary organisations.
- Pressure Groups.

- Local Community representatives.

Other issues

Other considerations are:

- Funding for contracts to be placed in the private sector will be dependent on the sales forecast. In the public sector, it tends to be based on annual budgeting, which is not ideally suited to long-term contracts. Budgets are regularly subject to review, both from within a department and also from changes imposed at the highest level in central government. Such changes are disruptive to the contract manager and the contractor and require flexibility in any long-term arrangement on the scope and ultimately the ability to end it through a termination for convenience clause.

- Public sector organisations tend to be risk averse and this factor impacts on contracting strategies. This may mean for example:
  - Longer periods of fixed prices.
  - Unwillingness to take on unlimited liabilities such as indemnities.
  - Only dealing with only large contractors ("nobody got fired for specifying IBM"!).
  - Sticking with the safe option, rather than being innovative.
- The sustainability agenda will be tend to be higher profile in the public sector as it is seen as driving force behind such changes. This will mean that the contract manager may be under greater pressure to consider such issues as:
  - Energy – reduction, renewable vs. fossil fuels.
  - Waste – reduction, reuse, recycling, landfill.
  - Economic Development.
  - Fair Trade.

- Carbon Dioxide emissions.
- Global issues; deforestation.
- Labour issues: child labour; employee rights.
- Small/Medium Enterprise agenda.
- Equal opportunities.

- There may also be policies within the public sector to promote activity within the third sector i.e. opening up contracting opportunities to VCOs such as the Citizens Advice Bureau or organisations that specialise in increasing the opportunities of disabled people such as Remploy. This can significant advantages:
  - Specialist skills and services may be available.
  - The provision can be very cost effective, especially where volunteers are employed.
  - There is independence from formal government organisations and flexibility and innovation can therefore be encouraged.
  - There are the wider benefits of citizen participation.

Chapter Summary

In this chapter, we have considered some of the major issues facing the contract manager in the public sector, comparing it with the private sector in particular with regard to objectives, compliance and perception.

13 Contract Close-out

Introduction

It is often tempting to believe that when a contract is complete, i.e. when the all of the items contracted for have been supplied or all the specified work is complete, it is time to relax. This however is not the case, as we have the following considerations.

- The need to ensure that both sides have met all of their obligations that were defined in the contract.

- Any outstanding financial issues have been resolved (e.g. with regard to claims and variations).

- Any post contractual obligations (such as guarantees, retention releases are being managed).

- The opportunity to review the performance of both the customer and contractor is taken.

In respect of the last point, we should be mindful of the famous quotation from George Santayana *"Those who cannot learn from history are doomed to repeat it."* Carrying out Lessons Learned exercises are often talked about, but less often put into practice.

Contractual Obligations

Actions required before completion

When it is believed a contract is complete, if it is a simple supply only contract, then assessing completion may be no more than signing of a final delivery note. For a services or works contract, this is likely to be more complex. Ascertaining completion by the customer may consist of examining the original contract specification and any subsequent variations and asking oneself, "Have I obtained what I contracted for?" or has the contractor for filled their contractual obligations.

This can be established in several ways:

- A physical inspection of the works. This will not only include the required deliverable, but also such issues as to whether the site has been left in a clean and tidy state.

- Reference to written specifications, drawings, programmes of work.

- Witnessing testing and plant commissioning programmes carried out by the contractor.

- Ensuring all necessary documentation required by the contract such as Test Certificates, Operation and Maintenance Manuals has been provided.

Signifying Completion

In order to ensure, that the contract is formally closed, so that both sides are aware of that their obligations have been completed and that any payments can be generated, the following is a model process than can be used, but can be varied to suit circumstances.

The contractor believing that he has completed the works can apply to the customer for a Taking-Over Certificate (this has many alternative names such as Takeover, Completion or Substantial Completion). This application will be sent to the customer who if satisfied that the works are complete will issue such a certificate. This is a significant contractual event, of which the consequences are:

- The customer now has control of the contract deliverable and the right to make use of the works.

- Responsibility for insurance now passes to the customer.

- The guarantee period normally commences.

- If the contract dictates, a payment may now be due or a retention required to be released.

The customer includes the final contract price on the certificate, but may also have the ability (depending on the terms of the contract) to highlight on this certificate, a list of minor items, which are required to remedied or completed, but are not so significant as to prevent taking-over. Items such as repairing some minor paint damage on a new building could fall into this category, whereas a leaking roof probably would not. This list is known variously as a Snagging, Exceptions or Punch list and should be included on or accompany this certificate.

When the guarantee period is complete, the contractor can then apply for a **Final Certificate** (this has many alternative names such as a Maintenance Certificate). This confirms that there are no further quality issues under the guarantee and depending upon the conditions of contract, may lead to the release a final retention.

After this point, the only redress to the customer is where they may be some statutory redress under Sales of Goods and Services Legislation. Any actions taken after issue of the Final Certificate would be subject to the Limitation Act, which limits any action through the courts to 6 years from the date of breach for a simple contract and 12 years for one let under seal. Unless there has been a significant breach of contract that could neither party could have been aware of during the running of the contract, this is unlikely to be viable option.

Where the contract has been complex and the final price includes a large number of variations, claims, time and materials works, incentivisation, commitment of optional work, concessions etc, it is possible that there may be some confusion as to its actual value. To ensure both sides are certain as to the final contract value, the contractor may apply for and the customer issue a **Final Account** which will break this down into the component parts listed above, which then add up to a final price. Such a document is often used for construction contracts and can reduce the possibility of disputes at a future time.

Late Completion

What happens if all of the work has been completed satisfactorily by the contractor, but the date is later than the originally specified in the contract? If the customer is responsible, then an extension to time may be granted and if the contractor has incurred any additional costs, then he may be entitled to an addition to the Contract Price, through a claim.

What happens however if the delay is caused by the contractor? If the contract is silent on this matter, then unless the contractor voluntarily accepts a reduction in price, then the recourse is through a dispute process and ultimately the courts. In such an instance the court would award what is known as **Damages at Large**, the value of which would be the loss the customer had to bear arising out the late completion. This is generally a very unsatisfactory solution as other than where a very large amount of money is involved, in most cases, the cost of litigation would substantially outweigh the value of damages claimed.

Therefore, the normal solution is to have a mechanism within the contract which allows for deduction from the contact, without the need for any dispute resolution process to be commenced. The most commonly used is Liquidated Damages which can be defined as genuine, pre-estimate of loss that would be incurred, where a breach (normally late completion) has been incurred. This definition helps us to understand the nature of such a clause:

- Genuine – the loss suffered by the customer must be one that would actually be suffered as a result of the late completion, such as :
  - Loss of income through non-availability of the items or service. For example, if parts are delivered late, then the subsequent product is not available for sale, until later than planned.
  - Additional internal costs incurred such as contract management and supervision of contractors working beyond the original completion date.
  - Claims paid to other contractors arising out of consequential delay.

  Note: Any attempt to impose a sum not related to a genuine loss or was disproportionate to the loss caused, would be deemed a Penalty Clause and would be unenforceable in English Law (though not necessarily in overseas countries).

- Pre-estimate – the formula for deduction must have been previously agreed within the Contract and not imposed, when the delay has occurred. Such a clause might be drafted as follows:
  - "Where the Contractor fails to complete the Works by the Contractual Completion Date, there shall be deducted from payments due to the Contractor, Liquidated Damages of 1% of the Contract Price for each day between Contractual Completion Date and the date of actual Taking Over, subject to a maximum limit of 20% of the Contract Price."
  - In this case a maximum limit has been set, as it is unlikely that a contractor would be willing to accept an unlimited liability and the courts may deem such

an arrangement as a penalty. There is a however potential for a contractor to believe that one the maximum has been reached, he is no longer under any further monetary pressure to complete.

- Other issues with Liquidated Damages include:
  - The intention is that they are not needed, as the contractor has a monetary incentive to complete on time.
  - There is a danger that a contractor who anticipates completing late may build their potential cost into his tender price.
  - Liquidated Damages do not just have to set against completion; they can be also be set against specific contract milestones.
  - If a customer intends to deduct Liquidated Damages, he should be prepared for a potential counter-claim as a contractor may look back at the history of the contract to see where the customer may have failed to meet his obligations.

Lessons Learnt

Why Lessons Learnt?

When all contractual issues have been resolved, it is time to reflect on what went well and what went badly on the contract. This is sometimes seen as a box-ticking exercise, but can be of great value to the both the customer and the contractor as both the customer and contractor can examine areas, where they displayed weakness in meeting their contractual obligations and use this information to improve, should they have or intend to have any future contractual relationships.

The customer can use the process to:

- Assemble a significant amount of performance data, which can then be used in any future tenderer selection exercises.

- Confirm to key stakeholders (such as its customers or regulators) that the organisation is committed to continuous improvement).

- Benchmark the performance of one contractor over several contracts or against other contractors employed by the customer.

- Improve its own processes through constructive feedback from the contractor.

In the same way the contractor can benefit through:
- Gaining valuable feedback to assist in future tender submissions and contract management processes, not just for this customer, but for his entire client base.

- A willingness to participate showing good faith and trust towards the customer.

Feedback Content

Provided that there is a good relationship between the customer and the contractor, the feedback process should be two-way on both of their performances. Where possible the feedback should be objective, measurable and if possible related to specific Key Performance Indicators written into the contract.

In some cases, there will be an element of subjectivity, but there should be at least some form of scaled measurement (e.g. for "responsiveness to queries", 1 = "Always had to be chased several times for a response" to 5 = "Gave immediate, good quality responses"). If this type of measurement is applied to all potential categories, an overall score can be calculated.

Contractor Performance – What to Measure Against

The customer should measure the performance of the contractor, who should also self-measure. There are many topics, which could be measured including:

Quality
- How far did the final product, service meet its specification?
- Where the contractor carried out design work, how far was it fit for purpose?

Delivery
- Did the contractor complete the works on time?
- Did the contractor manage the programme of works well or did he constantly need progressing?

Cost
- Did the contractor work within any cost targets or did he try to obtain additional monies through spurious claims or variations?
- Did to contractor propose and/or implement any cost saving opportunities?

Documentation
- Did the contractor submit required documentation on time and to a quality and format acceptable to the customer?
- Did the contractor conform to the requirements of an acceptable Quality Management System?

Health, Safety and Environment
- Were there any incidents involving injury to persons or damage to plant, buildings or the environment?
- Did the contractor display a positive attitude to continuous improvement to health, safety and environment processes?

Communication

- How willing was the contractor to communicate, particularly on "bad news" issues?
- How responsive was he to queries from the customer?

It would be expected that the customer would weight each of the categories used, depending on their relative importance in the contract. For example, one would expect a higher weighting given to Health, Safety and Environment on a demolition contract as opposed to a financial consultancy agreement.

Customer Performance – What to Measure Against

The contractor should measure the performance of the customer, who should also self-measure. One again, there are many topics, which could be measured including:

Quality

- How good was the customer's specification? Were there many variations issued, due to omissions, changes of mind or ambiguity?

Access

- Did the customer give access to the contractor to carry out work in accordance with the contract programme?

Documentation

- Did the customer issue documents such as permits for work, variations, payment certificates in a timely manner?
- Did the customer approve submissions from the contractor, such as designs, method statements, drawings in a timely manner?

Communication

- How willing was the customer to communicate, particularly on "bad news" issues?
- How responsive was he to queries from the contractor?

Format of Lesson Learnt Exercises

Ideally, there should be a Lessons Learnt Workshop, with participants from both the contractor and customer, though this would not be appropriate for low value, low risk contracts, where written correspondence may suffice. Where a Lessons Learnt Workshop is held, it is important that there is a high degree of trust and a willingness to be open and honest. Such meetings must not be used to:

- Re-open negotiations or a dispute on contractual matter.

- As a means of settling old scores or to put an individual "in their place".

- An opportunity for negative criticism.

It is important that both parties feel that they can be candid in their assessment and this will not prejudice any future relationships. In addition both parties must be committed to making any improvements arising out of this exercise and not be seen to be just going through the motions.

Chapter Summary

In this chapter, the key themes were ensuring that when a contract is closed out, all outstanding matters have been resolved, formal documentation is issued to facilitate payment and that any lessons learned are recorded and formally acted upon.

Contract Close Out

Index